College Admissions

Other Books in the Current Controversies Series

College Admissions

Dedria Bryfonski, Book Editor

GREENHAVEN PRESS
A part of Gale, Cengage Learning

GALE
CENGAGE Learning·

Farmington Hills, Mich • San Francisco • New York • Waterville, Maine
Meriden, Conn • Mason, Ohio • Chicago

Elizabeth Des Chenes, *Director, Content Strategy*
Douglas Dentino, *Manager, New Product*

© 2015 Greenhaven Press, a part of Gale, Cengage Learning

WCN: 01-100-101

For more information, contact:
Greenhaven Press
27500 Drake Rd.
Farmington Hills, MI 48331-3535
Or you can visit our Internet site at gale.cengage.com

Articles in Greenhaven Press anthologies are often edited for length to meet page requirements. In addition, original titles of these works are changed to clearly present the main thesis and to explicitly indicate the author's opinion. Every effort is made to ensure that Greenhaven Press accurately reflects the original intent of the authors. Every effort has been made to trace the owners of copyrighted material.

Cover image © Cynthia Farmer/Shutterstock.com.

LIBRARY OF CONGRESS CATALOGING-IN-PUBLICATION DATA

College Admissions / Dedria Bryfonski, book editor.
    pages cm. -- (Current controversies)
    Summary: "Current Controversies: College Admissions This series covers today's most current national and international issues and the most important opinions of the past and present. The purpose of the series is to introduce readers to all sides of contemporary controversies"-- Provided by publisher.
    Includes bibliographical references and index.
    ISBN 978-0-7377-7002-5 (hardback) -- ISBN 978-0-7377-7003-2 (paperback)
    1. Universities and colleges--United States--Admission--Juvenile literature. I. Bryfonski, Dedria.
    LB2351.2.C596 2014
    378.1'01--dc23
                                                                2014017888

Printed in the United States of America
1 2 3 4 5 6 7 18 17 16 15 14

Contents

Chapter 1: Should Race Be a Consideration in College Admissions?

Jeffrey M. Jones

Although a majority of Americans are in favor of the government taking an active role to help minorities, a poll showed that two-thirds of Americans believe colleges should admit students solely on the basis of merit. Researchers suggest that Americans may be reluctant to support a program that could potentially grant college admittance to unqualified students.

Yes: Race Should Be a Consideration in College Admissions

Lee C. Bollinger

Those who believe that a commitment to racial diversity on college campuses should be replaced with efforts to recruit more low-income students are misguided. Campuses are enriched by having students with a broad range of talents, experiences, and backgrounds. Adding more low-income students is a laudable goal, but it should not come at the expense of minority enrollment.

Michal Kurlaender and Eric Grodsky

The so-called mismatch theory is often cited by critics of affirmative action in college admissions. The theory claims that the beneficiaries of affirmative action are set up for failure because they are placed in academic environments that are too challenging for their current abilities. However, researchers at the University of California have demonstrated that allegedly mismatched students in fact do quite well and benefit from being in a challenging environment.

No: Race Should Not Be a Consideration in College Admissions

Using race as a determining factor in higher education admissions is prohibited by the Equal Protection Clause of the Fourteenth Amendment to the US Constitution. Essentially, the logic behind this form of discrimination is no different than that used by pro-segregationists during the 1950s. Furthermore, the race-conscious admissions system used by the University of Texas at Austin actually harms minorities by putting them in academic settings in which they are ill-prepared to compete.

Chapter 2: Should Colleges Consider Legacies in the Admissions Process?

80

A recent study of thirty top colleges revealed that being a legacy student increased the probability of admission by 23.3 percent overall and by 45 percent if the connection was a parent. The findings suggest that the benefit conveyed by legacy status is greater than previously believed.

Yes: Colleges Should Consider Legacies in the Admissions Process

85

Former president of George Washington University Stephen Joel Trachtenberg defends the practice of legacy admissions, arguing that legacy students bring with them a sense of tradition and school spirit that enriches campus life. Students with a strong desire to be at a particular school because of a family connection contribute to a positive campus culture.

88

Critics of legacy preference fail to consider the fact that the student displaced by a legacy student at one top university will get into another excellent institution and receive a good education. Private colleges need the donations of alumni members to retain their excellence, and preferential treatment to legacy students encourages alumni giving.

91

As admissions to competitive institutions such as Brown University are becoming more selective, legacy preferences have come under attack as favoring members of a white upper class. However, the reality is that a student's legacy status is only used as a tie-breaker between equally qualified candidates.

No: Colleges Should Not Consider Legacies in the Admissions Process

Legacy preferences benefit white students at the expense of minority students, because white students are more likely to have parents or other relatives who attended college in the past. Although some argue that legacy preferences benefit fundraising, this has been proven not to be the case. Therefore, legacy preferences are unconstitutional, because they negatively impact minorities without any offsetting benefit to the institution.

Chapter 3: Should Athletes Get Preferential Treatment in College Admissions?

Yes: Athletes Should Get Preferential Treatment in College Admissions

Libby Sander

Adrian College in Michigan was a private liberal-arts college with shrinking enrollment and a dubious future until it began aggressively recruiting athletes. Within three years, the institution increased its enrollment by almost 60 percent while becoming more selective in its admissions.

The Daily Princetonian

Despite the label of the "dumb jock," many college athletes are excellent students. Colleges benefit from having athletes on campus, as they frequently have different backgrounds and interests than traditional students.

Douglas Brennan

The trend of colleges offering fewer academic and more athletic scholarships makes economic sense for colleges. An excellent athletic program generates a significant amount of money that can be used by a college not only for sports but also for financial aid and investment projects.

No: Athletes Should Not Get Preferential Treatment in College Admissions

The special consideration that athletes receive in college admissions means that many young people focus on athletics rather than academics at an early age as a way into college. America would be better off if students were rewarded for their prowess in math and science, not athletics.

Students recruited to Division I colleges on athletic scholarships face significant challenges. Being an athlete in an elite program is extremely time-consuming and exacts a physical and emotional toll. They also must compete academically with a student body of high-achievers, while many college athletes are only average students. Given these facts, it is understandable why college athletes struggle to succeed as students.

Chapter 4: Should Standardized Tests Be a Factor in College Admissions?

Yes: Standardized Tests Should Be a Factor in College Admissions

Studies have shown that the SAT, paired with high school grade point average (GPA), is an accurate predictor of college success. Because the SAT is a national test, it provides an objective benchmark that is needed because of inconsistent grading from one high school to another.

A 2010 study has confirmed the findings of a previous study showing that the SAT favors white students over black because of cultural differences. Research suggests that white students tend to do better than blacks on the easier verbal questions, while black students perform better than whites on harder questions. The easier questions favor white students because they are based on the dominant white culture that these students have grown up in.

Foreword

By definition, controversies are "discussions of questions in which opposing opinions clash" (*Webster's Twentieth Century Dictionary Unabridged*). Few would deny that controversies are a pervasive part of the human condition and exist on virtually every level of human enterprise. Controversies transpire between individuals and among groups, within nations and between nations. Controversies supply the grist necessary for progress by providing challenges and challengers to the status quo. They also create atmospheres where strife and warfare can flourish. A world without controversies would be a peaceful world; but it also would be, by and large, static and prosaic.

The Series' Purpose

The purpose of the Current Controversies series is to explore many of the social, political, and economic controversies dominating the national and international scenes today. Titles selected for inclusion in the series are highly focused and specific. For example, from the larger category of criminal justice, Current Controversies deals with specific topics such as police brutality, gun control, white collar crime, and others. The debates in Current Controversies also are presented in a useful, timeless fashion. Articles and book excerpts included in each title are selected if they contribute valuable, long-range ideas to the overall debate. And wherever possible, current information is enhanced with historical documents and other relevant materials. Thus, while individual titles are current in focus, every effort is made to ensure that they will not become quickly outdated. Books in the Current Controversies series will remain important resources for librarians, teachers, and students for many years.

In addition to keeping the titles focused and specific, great care is taken in the editorial format of each book in the series. Book introductions and chapter prefaces are offered to provide background material for readers. Chapters are organized around several key questions that are answered with diverse opinions representing all points on the political spectrum. Materials in each chapter include opinions in which authors clearly disagree as well as alternative opinions in which authors may agree on a broader issue but disagree on the possible solutions. In this way, the content of each volume in Current Controversies mirrors the mosaic of opinions encountered in society. Readers will quickly realize that there are many viable answers to these complex issues. By questioning each author's conclusions, students and casual readers can begin to develop the critical thinking skills so important to evaluating opinionated material.

Current Controversies is also ideal for controlled research. Each anthology in the series is composed of primary sources taken from a wide gamut of informational categories including periodicals, newspapers, books, US and foreign government documents, and the publications of private and public organizations. Readers will find factual support for reports, debates, and research papers covering all areas of important issues. In addition, an annotated table of contents, an index, a book and periodical bibliography, and a list of organizations to contact are included in each book to expedite further research.

Perhaps more than ever before in history, people are confronted with diverse and contradictory information. During the Persian Gulf War, for example, the public was not only treated to minute-to-minute coverage of the war, it was also inundated with critiques of the coverage and countless analyses of the factors motivating US involvement. Being able to sort through the plethora of opinions accompanying today's major issues, and to draw one's own conclusions, can be a complicated and frustrating struggle. It is the editors' hope that Current Controversies will help readers with this struggle.

Introduction

> *"The playing field is not level—most elite universities give extra weight in the admissions process to underrepresented minorities, athletes, and the children of alumni."*

Some parents begin thinking about how to get their children into a competitive college the day they are born. In the process of writing *Playing to Win: Raising Children in a Competitive Culture*, sociologist Hilary Levey Friedman observed and interviewed ninety-five families with elementary school-age children involved in soccer, chess, and dance. Among the children she encountered was Jeremiah, an eight-year-old boy who attended a highly rated independent day school in the northeast United States. In the top fifty of competitive chess players in his age group in the country, Jeremiah also played competitive soccer and studied piano and music theory. Jeremiah's upbringing is similar to that of many middle-class and upper-middle-class children whose parents invest considerable time and money on the extracurricular activities of their offspring, the author observed. According to Friedman, "It would be a mistake to imagine that parents of young kids fixate on college admissions offices every Saturday out on the soccer field. But they do seem to expect that early grooming in the tournaments of sports or dance or chess will produce in their child the track record of success they need to ensure that thick admissions envelope when the time comes."[1]

In fall 2013, a record 21.8 million students were attending American colleges and universities. Of the approximately 3,700 colleges and universities, including more than two thousand

1. Hilary Levey Friedman, "Competitive Kids: College Admissions Game Starts Early," *Education Next*, Winter 2014. http://educationnext.org/competitive-kids.

four-year colleges in the United States, more than 80 percent accept over half of their applicants, according to statistics cited by Kat Cohen in "The Truth About College Acceptance Rates: How Low Can They Go?" in *The Huffington Post*. With the right research and realistic expectations, there is literally a college match for every student, Cohen maintains. However, there is a widespread perception that where a child goes to school has far-reaching consequences for future success. According to Friedman:

> The way people get into the upper-middle class and upper class now is based on educational credentials. If you're a doctor, lawyer, or MBA—you can't pass those on to your kids. You can't just pass on the family business anymore. Ivanka Trump went to Wharton. I'm sure her name helped, but she still had to go to Wharton. You have to get those credentials. And now, you have to do well in school but also distinguish yourself outside the classroom.[2]

According to Marjorie Hansen Shaevitz in *USA Today Magazine*, "Today there are more applicants and greater competition for the same number of admittance slots, especially at highly selective institutions."[3] At the top of the highly selective list is Stanford University, which accepted only 5.69 percent of its more than 38,800 applicants in 2013. Not far behind is Harvard University, accepting only 5.79 percent of its applicants. Others in the most competitive category with overall acceptance rates of under 15 percent include Amherst College, Bowdoin College, Columbia University, Pitzer College, and Pomona College.

However, admissions counselors often point to competitive colleges considered to offer an excellent education with overall

2. Quoted in Jessica Grose, "Are You Raising Your Kids 'to Win,'" *Slate*, August 29, 2013. http://www.slate.com/blogs/xx_factor/2013/08/29/playing_to_win_hilary_levey_fried man_s_new_book_on_our_activities_obsessed.html.
3. Marjorie Hansen Shaevitz, "Always Have a Backup,'" *USA Today Magazine*, March 2013.

acceptance rates over 50 percent. Among these are DePaul University, George Mason University, Ohio Wesleyan University, the University of Georgia, the University of Illinois at Urbana-Champaign, the University of Washington, and the University of Wisconsin.

Complicating the admissions situation is the fact that the playing field is not level—most elite universities give extra weight in the admissions process to underrepresented minorities, athletes, and the children of alumni. According to data from the National Study of College Experience of 124,374 applications for admission to elite universities during the 1980s and part of the 1990s, African American applicants received the equivalent of 230 extra SAT points (on a 1600 point scale), Hispanic students received an additional 185 points, recruited athletes 200 points, and legacy candidates 160 points. On the other end of the scale, the study found that Asian-American students had an average of 50 points deducted from their SAT scores.

In his article "The Admissions Race" in *The Amherst Student*, James Liu tells the story of his friend who had a perfect score of 2400 on the SAT Reasoning Test, perfect scores of 800 on two SAT Subject Tests, scores of 5 on eight AP exams, and a 4.0 grade point average. In addition, he held multiple club leadership positions. Despite all this, he was waitlisted and then ultimately rejected by Harvard University, Yale University, Princeton University, and Dartmouth College, his top four college choices. According to Liu's friend, "It's frustrating. It's absolutely frustrating to know that I was so close and that the smallest factor could have tipped the scales in my favor.... I know that I could've gotten in if only for that smallest factor ... if only I hadn't quit soccer, if only I had taken speech and debate more seriously or if only I hadn't been born Asian."[4] Popularly called the "bamboo curtain," the existence of Asian

4. James Liu, "The Admissions Race," *The Amherst Student*, April 24, 2013. http://amherststudent.amherst.edu/?q=article/2013/04/24/admissions-race.

quotas is an area of controversy in college admissions. According to Ron Unz, publisher of *The American Conservative*, in a *New York Times* article:

> Just as their predecessors of the 1920s always denied the existence of "Jewish quotas," top officials at Harvard, Yale, Princeton and the other Ivy League schools today strongly deny the existence of "Asian quotas." But there exists powerful statistical evidence to the contrary.
>
> Each year, American universities provide their racial enrollment data to the National Center for Educational Statistics, which makes this information available online. After the Justice Department closed an investigation in the early 1990s into charges that Harvard University discriminated against Asian-American applicants, Harvard's reported enrollment of Asian-Americans began gradually declining, falling from 20.6 percent in 1993 to about 16.5 percent over most of the last decade. This decline might seem small. But these same years brought a huge increase in America's college-age Asian population, which roughly doubled between 1992 and 2011, while non-Hispanic white numbers remained almost unchanged.[5]

Debating this position in the same edition of *The New York Times*, college admission and financial aid advisor Rod M. Bugarin Jr., wrote:

> Asian and Asian-American students should embrace affirmative action because it allows you to present yourself as a complete person instead of reducing yourself to a test score. More important, a campus composed only of students who have aced standardized tests cannot match the dynamic, diverse ethos that currently exists. I'm sure that many students, particularly Asian and Asian-Americans, would not

---

5. Ron Unz, "Statistics Indicate an Ivy League Asian Quota," *New York Times*, December 19, 2012 (updated December 3, 2013). http://www.nytimes.com/roomfordebate/2012/12/19/fears-of-an-asian-quota-in-the-ivy-league/statistics-indicate-an-ivy-league-asian-quota.

find Ivy League schools as desirable if their campus communities only valued competitive high-stakes testing where only a few are given the opportunity to succeed.[6]

Applying to college is typically an anxiety-producing experience for high school students and their parents, with the anxiety exacerbated by the issues surrounding the process. The viewpoints of educators, journalists, and other commentators are presented in the following four chapters of this book: "Should Race Be a Consideration in College Admissions?," "Should Colleges Consider Legacies in the Admissions Process?," "Should Athletes Get Preferential Treatment in College Admissions?," and "Should Standardized Tests Be a Factor in College Admissions?"

6. Rod M. Bugarin Jr., "Scores Aren't the Only Qualification," *New York Times*, December 19, 2012. http://www.nytimes.com/roomfordebate/2012/12/19/fears-of-an-asian-quota-in-the-ivy-league/scores-arent-the-only-qualification.

Should Race Be a Consideration in College Admissions?

In U.S., Most Reject Considering Race in College Admissions

Jeffrey M. Jones

Jeffrey M. Jones is managing editor for The Gallup Poll.

Two-thirds of Americans believe college applicants should be admitted solely based on merit, even if that results in few minorities being admitted, while 28% believe an applicant's racial and ethnic background should be taken into account to promote diversity on college campuses. Three-quarters of whites and 59% of Hispanics believe applicants should be judged only on merit, while blacks are divided in their views.

The Supreme Court has heard cases that challenged affirmative action programs in college admissions in recent years. In 2003, it declared unconstitutional the University of Michigan's undergraduate admissions process that automatically awarded minority applicants extra "points" in its admissions formula, but upheld the university's law school admissions process that took race into account more generally when evaluating each individual applicant. This year, it vacated and remanded a lower-court ruling on a challenge to the University of Texas' admissions program from a white applicant denied admission.

Gallup has asked about using race in college admissions decisions twice before, in 2003 just prior to the ruling in the University of Michigan case, and again in 2007. Americans' opinions have been quite stable over the past 10 years.

Aside from blacks, a majority of all other major subgroups believe colleges should determine admissions solely on merit.

But the percentage holding that view varies. For example, 87% of Republicans and 53% of Democrats prefer race-neutral admissions decisions. Also, those with postgraduate education are much more willing to have schools consider race and ethnicity in admissions than are those with less formal education.

Americans Support Affirmative Action in General

Even though Americans largely reject the idea of using race as a factor in college admissions, they still support affirmative action programs more generally. A separate question in the poll finds 58% of Americans saying they favor "affirmative action programs for racial minorities," including 51% of whites, 76% of blacks, and 69% of Hispanics.

Americans support the government's playing at least a minor role in trying to improve the social and economic position of blacks and other minority groups in the U.S.

There are large partisan differences in support for affirmative action—Democrats are twice as likely as Republicans to favor affirmative action programs. Republicans are one of only a few groups that show majority opposition. Whereas there were significant differences by education with regard to college admissions, there are only minor differences with regard to affirmative action programs in general.

Americans may be less likely to support affirmative action in college admissions because the question raises a potential specific consequence of such programs—admitting some minority students who would otherwise not be admitted on their merits alone—which could in their minds outweigh the positive aspects of the policy mentioned in the question. The general question on affirmative action, asked prior to the question on college admissions, does not discuss any pros or cons of affirmative action, suggesting Americans mostly have a positive reaction to the concept or term.

Racial Groups Differ on Government Role in Helping Minorities

Americans support the government's playing at least a minor role in trying to improve the social and economic position of blacks and other minority groups in the U.S., with 32% favoring a major government role and 44% a minor one. However, white Americans generally favor a minor government role, while most blacks and Hispanics prefer more significant government involvement.

The substantial racial differences have always been apparent in this question. But whites are now less likely to favor a major government role in assisting minorities than they were during the Bush administration. Blacks, though still supportive of a major government role, are also a bit less likely now than they were in 2004–2005 to think that. As a result, Hispanics now edge out blacks as the group most likely to favor a major government role in aiding minorities.

Implications

Americans are not averse to having the government take steps to help improve the conditions of minority groups in the United States, and in a broad sense express support for affirmative action programs. One of the clearest examples of affirmative action in practice is colleges' taking into account a person's racial or ethnic background when deciding which applicants will be admitted. Americans seem reluctant to endorse such a practice, and even blacks, who have historically been helped by such programs, are divided on the matter.

The Supreme Court has ruled some college admissions practices unconstitutional for violating the guarantee of equal protection under the law. But the Court also said affirmative action in college admissions is permissible if it stands up to "strict scrutiny," agreeing that the goal of a diverse student body is worthy but race should be one of many factors taken into account rather than being a determining factor.

The recent University of Texas case suggests the issue is far from settled, and individuals denied admission may continue to go to court to challenge admissions procedures at other schools to see if their programs appropriately balance equal protection under the law versus achieving the goals of a diverse student body and helping raise the economic position of minorities.

Both Racial and Class Diversity Benefit College Campuses

Lee C. Bollinger

Lee C. Bollinger is the president of Columbia University. He was the president of the University of Michigan during two affirmative action cases that made their way to the US Supreme Court, Grutter v. Bollinger *and* Gratz v. Bollinger *and is considered a staunch defender of affirmative action.*

The distance the United States has traveled in overcoming racial discrimination reflects one of our nation's greatest achievements. Our long struggle toward redeeming the country's founding ideal of equality has been embraced for decades by virtually every institutional sector in American society. But we still have a long way to go. And with an imminent Supreme Court ruling in *Fisher v. University of Texas at Austin* [the US Supreme Court issued its decision in *Fisher v. University of Texas at Austin* on June 24, 2013, stipulating that a university's use of race must meet "strict scrutiny," that there is no other means of insuring a diverse student population], a case in which a white student has challenged the school's affirmative action policy, we are at risk of historical amnesia, of unraveling a heroic societal commitment that we have yet to fulfill. This is occurring amid a public debate too often framed by a false choice about diversity in higher education.

A Diverse Campus Has Real Benefits to Students

On university and college campuses, the educational benefits of racial and ethnic diversity are not theoretical but real and proven repeatedly over time. This is a conclusion embraced both by the Supreme Court in its definitive 2003 ruling on the matter, *Grutter v. Bollinger* (as University of Michigan's president at the time, I was the named defendant), and by my colleagues at 13 schools which, along with Columbia, jointly submitted a brief in the *Fisher* case asserting that "diversity encourages students to question their assumptions, to understand that wisdom and contributions to society may be found where not expected, and to gain an appreciation of the complexity of the modern world." Empirical studies have demonstrated that exposure to a culturally diverse campus community environment has a positive impact on students with respect to their critical thinking, enjoyment of reading and writing, and intellectual curiosity. Indeed, there is a nearly universal consensus in higher education about these benefits.

For many years now, the value of diverse backgrounds and viewpoints has been embraced as essential to the fabric of our major institutions, from the military services to private corporations. Yet there is evidence that, particularly in the private sector, the commitment to racial diversity is eroding. A change in the law at this moment making it harder for colleges and universities to supply racially diverse professional talent could be devastating.

There is widespread discomfort in this country with government or institutional policies that factor race into decision-making.

Yet, today, we are hearing the argument that higher education's historic commitment to racial diversity must be replaced by efforts to enroll more children of low-income families at top universities—as though these are mutually exclusive goals. The obvious reply is that the right course is to pursue both. Certainly at Columbia, we take great pride in an undergraduate student body with as high a percentage of low-

and moderate-income students as any of our peer institutions and the largest number of military veterans, as well as the highest percentage of African American students among the nation's top 30 universities. Over and over, our students tell us that they come for the intellectual excitement produced by the various kinds of diversity on our campus. In fact, last week at commencement when I addressed Columbia's class of 2013, the loudest applause from the graduates came in response to my suggestion that encountering the diversity of their talented classmates was the most influential part of their experience on campus.

Many other universities and colleges are equally committed to creating educational communities that reflect the widest possible ranges of talent, background, and human experience. For those of us whose job is to preserve and enhance the quality of higher education, the new insistence on choosing either socioeconomic or racial diversity makes no more sense than deciding that we can dispense with exposing our students to Alexis de Tocqueville's *Democracy in America* because they've already read Adam Smith's *Wealth of Nations*. To view them in the alternative is willfully and unnecessarily to impoverish the educational mission.

How, then, has this binary choice, at once voluntary and wrongheaded, come to inform the latest round of American society's recurring discussion of race, discrimination, and diversity?

The United States Is Far from Post-Racial

To start, there is widespread discomfort in this country with government or institutional policies that factor race into decision-making. One concern, a legitimate one, is that this door swings both ways: By opening it in order to use racial identity for benign purposes, such as overcoming past discrimination or promoting diversity, we also make ourselves vulnerable to institutionalized prejudice and bias.

The real challenges intrinsic to gaining diversity's many benefits must not be conflated, however, with the very different and erroneous idea that the United States in 2013 has become a post-racial society, for that surely is not the case. According to the Civil Rights Project at UCLA, the nation's population of African American and Latino K-12 students is more segregated than at any time since the 1960s. One-third of black students and almost one-half of white students attend a primary or secondary school where 90 percent of their classmates are of their race, a trend that shows no signs of abating. Particularly for these students, a college experience of immersion in a diverse student body will be essential if they are to thrive in the multi-racial society they will inhabit as adults.

Another familiar argument for ending affirmative action in higher education, cloaked in new data and rhetoric, is that such efforts put African American and Hispanic students in educational environments where they are over their heads and bound to fail. However well intended, this "mismatch theory" has been widely criticized by scholars for employing flawed methodology. Indeed, if there is one thing that respected studies have shown, it is that both minority and low-income students who went to top-tier colleges do better later in life than equally smart students who did not.

If we were to reverse course, we would find ourselves living in a changed and diminished America, where the number of black and Latino students admitted to the nation's top schools would be much smaller.

Racial Diversity Should Not Be Sacrificed for Class Diversity

Finally, it is understandable that public concern about high tuition costs and growing student debt has focused attention on maintaining socioeconomic diversity. But let's be candid. The source of increased tuition is not too much racial and cultural diversity; nor will the problem be solved by ending affirmative action in admissions. The real culprit here is the foolish decision of too many state governments to slash investment in public universities, like the one I graduated from, where the vast majority of students in the U.S. receive their college education and find a ladder of opportunity.

America's race problem was centuries in the making and is far from solved. This is not the moment for reversing our collective progress by limiting the ability of institutions of higher education to achieve racial diversity along with class diversity, and other forms as well.

If we were to reverse course, we would find ourselves living in a changed and diminished America, where the number of black and Latino students admitted to the nation's top schools would be much smaller. At California's flagship state universities, UCLA and Berkeley, the percentage of admitted undergraduate students who are African American is still 40 percent below what it was 17 years ago when the state adopted a referendum banning any consideration of race in the admissions process. The figures for admission of Latino applicants are better only because of the huge increase in the proportion of California's high school graduates who are Latino. Make no mistake: This outcome hurts all students on campus by robbing them of the skills learned through exposure to diverse people and perspectives, the very skills needed to succeed in today's global marketplace.

Should the Supreme Court make it impossible or difficult for colleges and universities to continue their affirmative action efforts, many will wonder why we saw fit to abandon our commitment to racial diversity in higher education. At that point the real mismatch will be painfully apparent—the one between the supposed gains brought about by banishing race from college admissions, and the reality produced by such a change.

Mismatch and the Paternalistic Justification for Selective College Admissions

Michal Kurlaender and Eric Grodsky

Michal Kurlaender is associate professor in the school of education at the University of California-Davis. Eric Grodsky is associate professor of sociology at the University of Wisconsin-Madison.

The legal battle over race-based affirmative action once again engaged the Supreme Court in 2013 via the *Fisher v. University of Texas* case. One of the Petitioner's central claims is that the pernicious effects of mismatch lead race-conscious admissions policies to harm minority students and "engender such high costs that they cannot be constitutionally justified" (American Educational Research Association 2012). However, how we identify mismatch, and how we conceive of its potential influence on both student outcomes and on the goals of public flagship institutions, remain open questions. . . .

The most important criteria for selection into competitive public and private colleges and universities are measures of prior academic achievement. These include a student's high school academic grade point average (GPA), scores on college entrance exams, and the rigor of the courses completed during high school. These criteria are motivated by two rationales. First, many believe that more prestigious colleges and universities make greater demands on their students than less competitive institutions. Students whose secondary school record place them substantially below their college peers are said to be "overmatched" and therefore at greater risk of aca-

Michal Kurlaender and Eric Grodsky, "Mismatch and the Paternalistic Justification for Selective College Admissions," *Center for Demography and Ecology Working Paper No. 2013-06*, May 2013. Copyright © 2013 by Sage Publications. Reproduced by permission.

demic failure or attrition than they would be at a less demanding college or university. According to this logic, it is in the student's own interest to attend a college at which she is about average, or at least not too far below average (Manski and Wise 1983). We refer to this viewpoint as the *paternalistic justification* for exclusion. . . .

The Paternalistic Justification and the Overmatch Hypothesis

The paternalistic justification gives rise to the overmatch hypothesis, which asserts that students are harmed by attending colleges and universities at which their level of prior academic achievement is substantially below the mean (Light and Strayer 2000; Sander and Taylor Jr. 2012; Thernstrom and Thernstrom 1997). This justification for exclusion is frequently employed by critics of race-based affirmative action who posit that beneficiaries of affirmative action are actually hurt by the policies; they are mismatched with the demands of the university and ultimately pay a penalty through academic failure, dropout, or weaker employment opportunities down the road (Clegg and Thompson 2012; Thernstrom and Thernstrom 1997; Will 2011). . . .

Testing the Mismatch Hypothesis at the University of California

In this paper we revisit the mismatch hypothesis, taking advantage of a unique natural experiment that occurred at UC in 2004. At that time the UC was comprised of eight campuses, three that we consider highly selective (Berkeley, Los Angeles, and San Diego) and five that we consider moderately selective (Davis, Irvine, Riverside, Santa Barbara, and Santa Cruz).[1] Of the three campuses we consider highly selective, *Barron's* ranked two as "most competitive" in 2004 and the other (San Diego) as "highly competitive" (Schmitt 2009). The average acceptance rate of our highly selective campuses was 30% in that year, compared to 59% for our moderately selective campuses.[2]

Until recently, the UC sought to admit all students it regarded as "UC eligible," though not necessarily to the campus of their choice. To be UC eligible students must earn a minimum grade-point average on a specified set of high school courses (known as a-g courses) and exceed threshold scores on standardized admissions tests (SAT or ACT) (Douglass 1999). In 2004, however, as a result of state budget cuts, several thousand students eligible to attend UC were denied immediate admission to the University. Instead, these students were offered admission through the Guaranteed Transfer Option (GTO) program, guaranteeing them future admission to a *specific campus* conditional on successfully completing lower-division requirements at a California Community College. The highly selective campuses in particular were urged by the Office of the President to reconsider students that they initially rejected and they complied, offering GTO admission to 2,300 students. When the state budget was restored that summer, GTO students were offered immediate admission (or admission in the next term) to the campus promised to them under GTO. . . .

Mismatched students attending an elite UC campus are no more likely to leave in their first 4 years prior to earning a degree than are regularly admitted students.

This unusual process resulted in the eventual admission of the GTO group to several highly selective UC institutions and presents a "natural experiment" in which the most selective campuses admitted applicants they originally rejected. These students are the most marginal admits—marginal on both observed attributes and attributes unobserved to the analyst. . . .

Exploiting this highly unusual admissions experiment, we asked what outcomes we would expect of the GTO students had they not been admitted to these competitive schools but instead attended less competitive UC campuses. The unique identification of these marginal admits freed us from relying on the standard parametric assumptions and statistical corrections for unobserved factors that lead students to choose schools and schools to choose students. On the student side, we observed a rich set of academic and socioeconomic characteristics, as well as the full UC application set, while on the institution side we had a natural experiment in admissions under which we could observe which matriculating students were least desirable from the perspective of the institution. . . .

Denying opportunities to students on the basis of a mismatch . . . is not clearly in the best interests of excluded students.

In this paper we operationalize "collegiate success" in three ways: GPA, credit accumulation, and persistence in the university 4 years from starting. Using a unique natural experiment in the admissions practices of three elite, highly selective UC campuses, we identified mismatched students as those not initially admitted but promised a spot after the UC Office of the President intervened. We showed that these students have academic profiles that are weaker than the academic profiles of the substantial majority of regularly admitted students to the elite universities, and more similar to (but still somewhat lower than) students admitted to other less competitive UC campuses. We used the regular admit pools to consider two comparison groups: (1) the better prepared students admitted in the first round by the elite UCs, and (2) students observationally similar to the GTOs attending institutions potentially better suited to our focal students—universities at which they would not be (as severely) mismatched.

Descriptively, the mismatch hypothesis appears to be at least partially true. Mismatched students attending elite schools earn lower average grades, are slightly slower to accrue credits, and are more likely to leave without a degree than regularly admitted students attending elite schools. Not surprisingly, much of the observed disadvantage GTO students face compared with their traditionally admitted classmates at elite schools is mediated by differences in academic achievement, social background, application patterns, and major. However, we argue that these background differences are not the same as mismatch; even "matched" students vary in their academic qualifications in ways that predict variation in postsecondary outcomes. Net of measured academic and social background, the average GPA of GTO students is only about 0.01 points lower than that of traditionally admitted elite students. Mismatched students accrue about seven fewer credits over their first 4 years of college than their regularly admitted elite peers, the equivalent of one to two courses, but, again, prior academic preparation and social background account for this modest difference. Perhaps most importantly, mismatched students attending an elite UC campus are no more likely to leave in their first 4 years prior to earning a degree than are regularly admitted students net of background characteristics. . . .

In this study we broadened the focus of mismatch beyond persistence to include grades and credit accumulation. We found that mismatch has no reliable or substantively notable bearing on grades, rates of credit accumulation, or persistence. Given the benefits that accrue to those who earn degrees from elite institutions, we reject the paternalistic justification for exclusion. Denying opportunities to students on the basis of a mismatch, at least within the rather substantial range of student background attributes we observe, is *not* clearly in the best interests of excluded students.

Notes

1. The first cohort to enter UC's ninth campus, Merced, started in 2005.

2. Authors' calculation based on UC Office of the President. 2010. "Final summary of freshman applications, admissions and enrollment, fall 1989-2009." (http://www.ucop.edu/news/factsheets/flowfrc_09.pdf).

The Minorities Admitted to Elite Institutions Have High Academic Qualifications

Sasanka Jinadasa

Sasanka Jinadasa attended Harvard University and is an intern at the Center for American Progress.

I don't think you are a bad person. I don't want to attack you. I believe, unlike many *Crimson* commenters, that you are qualified to attend this school. I have no reason to attack your intelligence, your presence here at Harvard, or your existence as a human being at all.

That said, your column in the *Crimson* two weeks ago made me angry [the author is referring to a column by Sarah Siskind published in the *Harvard Crimson* that argued against using race as a consideration in college admissions]. Not just angry for myself, a woman of color who has benefitted from multiple types of affirmative action, but for the communities I am perceived to be a part of, and for the communities that you believe have unfairly taken sitting room at our university.

Race Is Only One of Many Factors Considered

You flippantly argue that "adorable gingers" aren't considered a minority, in order to invalidate all minority groupings. Although, of course, there has been no systematic discrimination against gingers as a group throughout this nation's history, entrenched within governmental institutions and corporations alike. When there is evidence that gingers are routinely passed over during job interviews or that they are ensconced in a cycle of poverty, let me know, please.

Did you research for this article? I'm sure you did, but you must have missed that women are traditionally included within affirmative action policies. While Harvard itself has no gender-based affirmative action, perhaps the campaign should be to include it, not to eliminate race-based affirmative action.

If this is about resources, you argue, why don't we use *class-based* affirmative action? There are rich minorities! They have access to resources! Yes, they do. However, to act as if race doesn't uniquely affect one's pathway in life is simply untrue. Your view is not uncommon—whites commonly believe that it is lack of will rather than discrimination that keeps blacks from succeeding, while blacks report the opposite. Studies show again and again that blacks with exactly the same resumes as whites are often passed over in favor of their white counterparts. Blacks and whites are still gently pushed towards residential segregation, and these largely black neighborhoods become stuck in a cycle of poverty with poorer schools, fewer work options, and a smaller budget for local government.

Affirmative action is not discrimination, but an understanding of the role race plays in our society.

Harvard doesn't admit applicants with low academic qualifications. Please understand that. Their average standardized test scores (however flawed these are), average GPAs [grade point averages], and other quantitative measures are the highest in the nation. Black students and other students of color aren't dragging these averages back, and they aren't simply let in because of their race. Race is simply a factor to be considered as a potential marker of diversity and struggle against adversity. Students of color, upon attending this university, are required to take the same classes, pass the same exams, comp the same activities. The visually impaired are not capable of becoming pilots, but surely students of color are capable of taking tests.

I'm sorry that you have had the terrible disadvantage of psychological trauma regarding your privileged status at this university. Your affirmative action has little to do with structural inequality or diversity, but with cycles of money and legacy. I'm glad that your father donates money to this university; that is part of the reason I can afford to attend Harvard. I'm happy that you boosted Harvard's yield rate, as that is part of the reason they admitted you. I'm also glad that they admitted me, both as a qualified applicant, and to increase diversity on campus. I know that both of our affirmative actions are tactics. I understand that as a university, such tactics are practiced to improve both the image and the quality of the university. What you don't seem to understand, Sarah, is that this university has made a decision to create an environment of diverse vibrancy, where athletes and legacies and students of color all have a place. Academics are not the only reason students are admitted to Harvard—talent, potential for success, penchant for social change, these are all traits that a Harvard student might have. If Harvard admitted only students with SAT scores above a 2350, I guarantee that Harvard would not be an institution worth attending.

A Diverse Campus Benefits All Students

I, personally, don't care that there are Democrats who don't support affirmative action. There are also plenty of anti-choice, anti-marriage equality, and anti-welfare Democrats. They don't have my vote. However, to quote Supreme Court Chief Justice Roberts in the same paragraph as talking about partisan issues is laughable. "The only way to stop discrimination based on race is to stop discriminating based on race," he says. Affirmative action is not discrimination, but an understanding of the role race plays in our society. This is not a post-racial America, and refusing to think critically about race doesn't erase discrimination, it embeds it.

Of course, the Fourteenth Amendment prohibits race-based discrimination. What it doesn't prohibit is affirmative action, which in the modern day promotes the holistic review of an application, taking race into account as one of the many factors contributing to a person's unique situation in life. It affirms that their race has genuinely affected their perception of society, and society's perception of them.

Affirmative action serves its purpose, to create a campus where you can interact with students from many different backgrounds, colors, and creeds.

While you affirm that racism exists, you believe that affirmative action will affect how employers review the applications of those who have benefitted from it. However, I disagree with you: employers are not impressed that someone got into Harvard University, because all that reflects were your accomplishments in high school. Employers are impressed by the success that one has at an institution like Harvard, because that is what matters. My accomplishments at Harvard are what will go on my resume when I apply for jobs in two years, and it is my Harvard degree, not my Harvard acceptance, that will stand out.

I am succeeding at this university. I am surrounded by students of color who are thriving in spite of the barriers they were born with, and who are grateful for the opportunities they are given. We know that we are the lucky ones; we know that we are part of a select few that got an opportunity that many of our brothers and sisters of color will never have. I am aware of my privileges as a Harvard student.

Remember that you are lucky as well. You were lucky to be born in a family who cared about your education, and you are privileged to attend this university. Only 1700 make it out of more than 30,000 applications, and no one makes it here on merit alone. Affirmative action serves its purpose, to create a campus where you can interact with students from many different backgrounds, colors, and creeds, and the majority of people in the United States don't enjoy that privilege.

Affirmative action has benefitted your life, Sarah. I hope that you will take the opportunity to revel in the privileges it has granted you here at Harvard.

Best,

Sasanka Jinadasa

As Nonwhites Gain in Numbers, Improving Their Education Benefits Society

Ronald Brownstein

Ronald Brownstein is editorial director for strategic partnerships at Atlantic Media and writes a weekly column for the National Journal.

The lines of argument over affirmative action have changed little since the idea first combusted into controversy in the 1970s. But as the Supreme Court nears another critical ruling on the issue [in its ruling on *Fisher v. University of Texas at Austin*, issued June 24, 2013], the social and demographic context for these arguments has been transformed in ways that make the choices both more complex and consequential.

Minorities Make Up a Growing Segment of the Population

The Supreme Court issued its landmark ruling on higher-education affirmative action in the 1978 Bakke case, when it invalidated a numerical quota system for minority admissions at the University of California medical school but famously allowed colleges and universities to consider race as a "plus factor" in admission. Since then, the Court has further tightened but not entirely banned the use of race in higher-education admissions—a pattern most observers expect the justices to continue when they rule soon on the latest dispute.

The *Fisher v. University of Texas* case has followed the familiar grooves from Bakke, with supporters of Abigail Fisher, the rejected white applicant, decrying "reverse discrimination" and the school's backers championing diversity and remediation of prior discrimination. Yet these arguments are landing in a nation facing a radically reconfigured racial reality. Listening to them in today's America is like trying to play an eight-track tape on an iPad.

When the Supreme Court decided Bakke, whites still made up 80 percent of America's population, including almost three-fourths of those under 18. But minorities now constitute more than 36 percent of the total population and are on track to become a majority of the youth population before 2020.

Inevitably, this demographic wave has crested into the academy. Federal figures show that nonwhites comprised 47 percent of the 2011 class entering higher education, up from one-third in 1996. The problem is that those overall numbers mask the emergence of what Anthony Carnevale and Jeff Strohl of Georgetown University's Center on Education and the Workforce have called a "de facto [in fact] dual system" of higher education in which minorities and low-income kids are funneling mostly into the least selective (and least rewarding) schools.

As Carnevale and Strohl have documented, from 1994 to 2006 African-American and Hispanic students increased from one-fifth to one-third of the enrollment at community colleges, and from one-sixth to two-fifths at the four-year schools rated least selective. Yet in the upper-rung universities considered "very" or "most" competitive, the combined black/Hispanic share remained stuck at only about 12 percent. Whites, meanwhile, plummeted as a share of all high-school seniors but still make up 75 percent of students in the most selective schools, almost unchanged from 78 percent in 1994. Likewise, youths from the top quarter of highest-earning families filled just over two-thirds of the seats at the most selective universities in 2006, slightly more than in 1982.

This sorting matters so much because more-selective institutions spend much more money per student and produce better results for them on every important measure—from graduation rates to starting salaries. The cumulative effect is that while higher education still allows individual students to fulfill the American Dream of climbing from humble origins, as a system it now mostly stratifies America's economic and racial inequalities.

The goal of democratizing opportunity in a diversifying society remains urgent—and unmet.

The United States Needs Well-Educated Minorities

In the Bakke era, affirmative action was justified mostly on grounds of fairness—the need to remedy past discrimination by opening doors historically closed to minorities. But amid America's demographic transformation, the allocation of higher-education opportunities now raises different issues of competitiveness and social stability. With the absolute number of whites in the workforce expected to decline through 2030, the U.S. will struggle to compete if it cannot move more low-income and minority youths through college. And a society that relies on minorities to fill most of its future workforce needs but reserves the best opportunities primarily for the children of white, college-educated parents will court endemic social tension.

With educational opportunity already stratifying by race and class, this seems an inopportune time to retrench affirmative action. But even if those programs survive, they cannot reverse these trends alone. Whatever the Court decides, the challenge of hardening inequality in higher education demands further responses. One option is replicating programs (like those in Texas and California) that guarantee public-university admission to the top graduates in all high schools (which lifts students from economically or racially segregated communities). The Century Foundation, in a recent report [May 23, 2013], spotlighted another key: strengthening community colleges, which remain the first rung for many less-advantaged students, and prodding top universities to accept more transfers from them. To improve social mobility, argues the foundation's Richard Kahlenberg, "it's more important to improve community colleges than to have a victory in the affirmative-action wars."

In the Fisher case, those wars' latest skirmish, the Supreme Court ultimately is ruling on a tactic not a goal. And however the Court treats the tactic of affirmative action, the goal of democratizing opportunity in a diversifying society remains urgent—and unmet. "We've got to step on the accelerator here," says Amy Wilkins, a senior adviser at the College Board. "We certainly can't stall out or back up."

Affirmative Action Is Racial Discrimination

Clarence Thomas

Clarence Thomas is an associate justice of the Supreme Court of the United States and the second African American to serve on the court.

I join the Court's opinion because I agree that the Court of Appeals did not apply strict scrutiny to the University of Texas at Austin's (University) use of racial discrimination in admissions decisions. I write separately to explain that I would overrule *Grutter v. Bollinger,* and hold that a State's use of race in higher education admissions decisions is categorically prohibited by the Equal Protection Clause.

Strict Scrutiny Applies to Racial Consideration

The Fourteenth Amendment provides that no State shall "deny to any person . . . the equal protection of the laws." The Equal Protection Clause guarantees every person the right to be treated equally by the State, without regard to race. "At the heart of this [guarantee] lies the principle that the government must treat citizens as individuals, and not as members of racial, ethnic, or religious groups." *Missouri v. Jenkins.* "It is for this reason that we must subject all racial classifications to the strictest of scrutiny."

Under strict scrutiny, all racial classifications are categorically prohibited unless they are "'necessary to further a compelling governmental interest'" and "narrowly tailored to that end." *Johnson v. California.* . . .

Clarence Thomas, "Fisher vs. University of Texas at Austin et al," June 24, 2013, U.S. Supreme Court.

The Benefits of Diversity Are Not Compelling

The University claims that the District Court found that it has a compelling interest in attaining "a diverse student body and the educational benefits flowing from such diversity." The use of the conjunction, "and," implies that the University believes its discrimination furthers two distinct interests. The first is an interest in attaining diversity for its own sake. The second is an interest in attaining educational benefits that allegedly flow from diversity.

Attaining diversity for its own sake is a nonstarter. As even *Grutter* recognized, the pursuit of diversity as an end is nothing more than impermissible "racial balancing." . . . Rather, diversity can only be the *means* by which the University obtains educational benefits; it cannot be an end pursued for its own sake. Therefore, the *educational benefits* allegedly produced by diversity must rise to the level of a compelling state interest in order for the program to survive strict scrutiny.

The putative educational benefits of student body diversity cannot justify racial discrimination.

Unfortunately for the University, the educational benefits flowing from student body diversity—assuming they exist—hardly qualify as a compelling state interest. Indeed, the argument that educational benefits justify racial discrimination was advanced in support of racial segregation in the 1950's, but emphatically rejected by this Court. And just as the alleged educational benefits of segregation were insufficient to justify racial discrimination then, see *Brown v. Board of Education*, the alleged educational benefits of diversity cannot justify racial discrimination today.

Discriminating Based on Race
Is Unconstitutional

Our desegregation cases establish that the Constitution prohibits public schools from discriminating based on race, even if discrimination is necessary to the schools' survival. In *Davis v. School Bd. of Prince Edward Cty*, decided with *Brown*, the school board argued that if the Court found segregation unconstitutional, white students would migrate to private schools, funding for public schools would decrease, and public schools would either decline in quality or cease to exist altogether. . . .

Unmoved by this sky-is-falling argument, we held that segregation violates the principle of equality enshrined in the Fourteenth Amendment. ("[I]n the field of public education the doctrine of 'separate but equal' has no place. Separate educational facilities are inherently unequal") . . . ("The fact that the schools might be closed if the order were enforced is no reason for not enforcing it. A person may not be denied enforcement of rights to which he is entitled under the Constitution of the United States because of action taken or threatened in defiance of such rights"). Within a matter of years, the warning became reality: After being ordered to desegregate, Prince Edward County closed its public schools from the summer of 1959 until the fall of 1964. Despite this fact, the Court never backed down from its rigid enforcement of the Equal Protection Clause's antidiscrimination principle.

In this case, of course, Texas has not alleged that the University will close if it is prohibited from discriminating based on race. But even if it had, the foregoing cases make clear that even that consequence would not justify its use of racial discrimination. It follows, *a fortiori* [with stronger reason], that the putative educational benefits of student body diversity cannot justify racial discrimination: If a State does not have a compelling interest in the *existence* of a university, it certainly cannot have a compelling interest in the supposed benefits that might accrue to that university from racial discrimination. . . .

Arguments for Affirmation Action Are Similar to Anti-Desegregation Arguments

It is also noteworthy that, in our desegregation cases, we rejected arguments that are virtually identical to those advanced by the University today. The University asserts, for instance, that the diversity obtained through its discriminatory admissions program prepares its students to become leaders in a diverse society. . . . The segregationists likewise defended segregation on the ground that it provided more leadership opportunities for blacks. . . . This argument was unavailing. It is irrelevant under the Fourteenth Amendment whether segregated or mixed schools produce better leaders. Indeed, no court today would accept the suggestion that segregation is permissible because historically black colleges produced Booker T. Washington, Thurgood Marshall, Martin Luther King, Jr., and other prominent leaders. Likewise, the University's racial discrimination cannot be justified on the ground that it will produce better leaders.

> *Educational benefits are a far cry from the truly compelling state interests that we previously required to justify use of racial classifications.*

The University also asserts that student body diversity improves interracial relations. . . . In this argument, too, the University repeats arguments once marshaled in support of segregation. . . . We flatly rejected this line of arguments in *McLaurin v. Oklahoma State Regents for Higher Ed.*, where we held that segregation would be unconstitutional even if white students never tolerated blacks. . . . It is, thus, entirely irrelevant whether the University's racial discrimination increases or decreases tolerance.

Finally, while the University admits that racial discrimination in admissions is not ideal, it asserts that it is a temporary necessity because of the enduring race consciousness of our society. . . . But these arguments too were unavailing. The Fourteenth Amendment views racial bigotry as an evil to be stamped out, not as an excuse for perpetual racial tinkering by the State. . . . The University's arguments to this effect are similarly insufficient to justify discrimination.

Racial Discrimination in Any Form Is Harmful

The University's arguments today are no more persuasive than they were 60 years ago. Nevertheless, despite rejecting identical arguments in *Brown*, the Court in *Grutter* deferred to the University's determination that the diversity obtained by racial discrimination would yield educational benefits. There is no principled distinction between the University's assertion that diversity yields educational benefits and the segregationists' assertion that segregation yielded those same benefits. . . . Educational benefits are a far cry from the truly compelling state interests that we previously required to justify use of racial classifications.

My view of the Constitution is the one advanced by the plaintiffs in *Brown*: "[N]o State has any authority under the equal-protection clause of the Fourteenth Amendment to use race as a factor in affording educational opportunities among its citizens." . . .

I would overrule *Grutter* and hold that the University's admissions program violates the Equal Protection Clause because the University has not put forward a compelling interest that could possibly justify racial discrimination.

While I find the theory advanced by the University to justify racial discrimination facially inadequate, I also believe that its use of race has little to do with the alleged educational benefits of diversity. I suspect that the University's program is instead based on the benighted notion that it is possible to tell when discrimination helps, rather than hurts, racial minorities. . . . The worst forms of racial discrimination in this Nation have always been accompanied by straight-faced representations that discrimination helped minorities.

Slaveholders argued that slavery was a "positive good" that civilized blacks and elevated them in every dimension of life. . . .

A century later, segregationists similarly asserted that segregation was not only benign, but good for black students. They argued, for example, that separate schools protected black children from racist white students and teachers. . . .

Following in these inauspicious footsteps, the University would have us believe that its discrimination is likewise benign. I think the lesson of history is clear enough: Racial discrimination is never benign. . . . The University's professed good intentions cannot excuse its outright racial discrimination any more than such intentions justified the now denounced arguments of slaveholders and segregationists.

As a result of the mismatching, many blacks and Hispanics . . . are placed in a position where underperformance is all but inevitable because they are less academically prepared than the white and Asian students with whom they must compete.

Overmatched Students Are Harmed

While it does not, for constitutional purposes, matter whether the University's racial discrimination is benign, I note that racial engineering does in fact have insidious consequences.

There can be no doubt that the University's discrimination injures white and Asian applicants who are denied admission because of their race. But I believe the injury to those admitted under the University's discriminatory admissions program is even more harmful.

Blacks and Hispanics admitted to the University as a result of racial discrimination are, on average, far less prepared than their white and Asian classmates. In the University's entering class of 2009, for example, among the students admitted outside the Top Ten Percent plan, blacks scored at the 52d percentile of 2009 SAT takers nationwide, while Asians scored at the 93d percentile. Blacks had a mean GPA of 2.57 and a mean SAT score of 1524; Hispanics had a mean GPA of 2.83 and a mean SAT score of 1794; whites had a mean GPA of 3.04 and a mean SAT score of 1914; and Asians had a mean GPA of 3.07 and a mean SAT score of 1991.

Tellingly, neither the University nor any of the 73 *amici* [friends] briefs in support of racial discrimination has presented a shred of evidence that black and Hispanic students are able to close this substantial gap during their time at the University. . . .

Furthermore, the University's discrimination does nothing to increase the number of blacks and Hispanics who have access to a college education generally. Instead, the University's discrimination has a pervasive shifting effect. The University admits minorities who otherwise would have attended less selective colleges where they would have been more evenly matched. But, as a result of the mismatching, many blacks and Hispanics who likely would have excelled at less elite schools are placed in a position where underperformance is all but inevitable because they are less academically prepared than the white and Asian students with whom they must compete. Setting aside the damage wreaked upon the self-confidence of these overmatched students, there is no evidence that they learn more at the University than they would have learned at other schools for which they were better prepared. Indeed, they may learn less.

Affirmative Action Is Harmful to Minorities

Richard Sander and Stuart Taylor Jr.

Richard Sander is a professor of law at the University of California at Los Angeles. An American journalist, Stuart Taylor Jr. is a columnist for The National Journal, *a contributing editor to* Newsweek, *and a frequent writer for* The Atlantic, Slate, The New Republic, *and* The Wall Street Journal.

A ffirmative action in university admissions started in the late 1960s as a noble effort to jump-start racial integration and foster equal opportunity. But somewhere along the decades, it has lost its way.

Racial Preferences Harm Minority Students

Over time, it has become a political lightning rod and one of our most divisive social policies. It has evolved into a regime of racial preferences at almost all selective schools—preferences so strikingly large and politically unpopular that administrators work hard to conceal them. The largest, most aggressive preferences are usually reserved for upper-middle-class minorities on whom they often inflict significant academic harm, whereas more modest policies that could help working-class and poor people of all races are given short shrift. Academic leaders often find themselves flouting the law and acting in ways that aggravate the worst consequences of large preferences. They have become prisoners of a system that many privately deplore for its often-perverse unintended effects but feel they cannot escape.

The single biggest problem in this system—a problem documented by a vast and growing array of research—is the tendency of large preferences to boomerang and harm their intended beneficiaries. Large preferences often place students in environments where they can neither learn nor compete effectively—even though these same students would thrive had they gone to less competitive but still quite good schools.

We refer to this problem as "mismatch," a word that largely explains why, even though blacks are more likely to enter college than are whites with similar backgrounds, they will usually get much lower grades, rank toward the bottom of the class, and far more often drop out. Because of mismatch, racial preference policies often stigmatize minorities, reinforce pernicious stereotypes, and undermine the self-confidence of beneficiaries, rather than creating the diverse racial utopias so often advertised in college campus brochures.

We have a terrible confluence of forces putting students in classes for which they aren't prepared, . . . while, at the same time, consolidating the stereotype that they are inherently poor students.

The mismatch effect happens when a school extends to a student such a large admissions preference—sometimes because of a student's athletic prowess or legacy connection to the school, but usually because of the student's race—that the student finds himself in a class where he has weaker academic preparation than nearly all of his classmates. The student who would flourish at, say, Wake Forest or the University of Richmond, instead finds himself at Duke, where the professors are not teaching at a pace designed for him—they are teaching to the "middle" of the class, introducing terms and concepts at a speed that is unnerving even to the best-prepared student.

The student who is underprepared relative to others in that class falls behind from the start and becomes increasingly lost as the professor and his classmates race ahead. His grades on his first exams or papers put him at the bottom of the class. Worse, the experience may well induce panic and self-doubt, making learning even harder.

When explaining to friends how academic mismatch works, we sometimes say: Think back to high school and recall a subject at which you did fine but did not excel. Suppose you had suddenly been transferred into an advanced class in that subject with a friend who was about at your level and 18 other students who excelled in the subject *and* had already taken the intermediate course you just skipped. You would, in all likelihood, soon be struggling to keep up. The teacher might give you some extra attention but, in class, would be focusing on the median student, not you and your friend, and would probably be covering the material at what, to you, was a bewildering pace.

Wouldn't you have quickly fallen behind and then continued to fall farther and farther behind as the school year progressed? Now assume that you and the friend who joined you at the bottom of that class were both black and everyone else was Asian or white. How would that have felt? Might you have imagined that this could reinforce in the minds of your classmates the stereotype that blacks are weak students?

Mismatched Students Contribute to Racial Stereotypes

So we have a terrible confluence of forces putting students in classes for which they aren't prepared, causing them to lose confidence and underperform even more while, at the same time, consolidating the stereotype that they are inherently poor students. And you can see how at each level there are feedback effects that reinforce the self-doubts of all the students who are struggling.

Of course, being surrounded by very able peers can confer benefits, too—the atmosphere may be more intellectually challenging, and one may learn a lot from observing others. We have no reason to think that *small* preferences are not, on net, beneficial. But contemporary racial preferences used by selective schools—especially those extended to blacks and Native Americans—tend to be extremely large, often amounting to the equivalent of hundreds of SAT points.

At the University of Texas, whose racial preference programs come before the Supreme Court for oral argument on October 10, [2012] the typical black student receiving a race preference placed at the 52nd percentile of the SAT; the typical white was at the 89th percentile. In other words, Texas is putting blacks who score at the middle of the college-aspiring population in the midst of highly competitive students. This is the sort of academic gap where mismatch flourishes. And, of course, mismatch does not occur merely with racial preferences; it shows up with large preferences of all types.

The willful denial of the mismatch issue is as big a problem as mismatch itself.

Research on the mismatch problem was almost non-existent until the mid-1990s; it has developed rapidly in the past half-dozen years, especially among labor economists. To cite just a few examples of the findings:

Black college freshmen are more likely to aspire to science or engineering careers than are white freshmen, but mismatch causes blacks to abandon these fields at twice the rate of whites.

Blacks who start college interested in pursuing a doctorate and an academic career are twice as likely to be derailed from this path if they attend a school where they are mismatched.

About half of black college students rank in the bottom 20 percent of their classes (and the bottom 10 percent in law school).

Black law school graduates are four times as likely to fail bar exams as are whites; mismatch explains half of this gap.

Interracial friendships are more likely to form among students with relatively similar levels of academic preparation; thus, blacks and Hispanics are more socially integrated on campuses where they are less academically mismatched.

Denying the Damage Done by Mismatch Creates a Problem

Given the severity of the mismatch problem, and the importance of diversity issues to university leaders, one might expect that understanding and addressing mismatch would be at the very top of the academic agenda.

But in fact it is a largely invisible issue. With striking uniformity, university leaders view *discussion* of the mismatch problem as a threat to affirmative action and to racial peace on campuses, and therefore a subject to be avoided. They suppress data and even often ostracize faculty who attempt to point out the seriousness of mismatch. (See, for instance, the case of UT professor Lino Graglia, who was condemned by university officials after he observed that black and Mexican-American students were "not academically competitive" with their white peers.) We believe that the willful denial of the mismatch issue is as big a problem as mismatch itself.

A powerful example of these problems comes from UCLA [University of California at Los Angeles], an elite school that used large racial preferences until the Proposition 209 ban took effect in 1998. The anticipated, devastating effects of the ban on preferences at UCLA and Berkeley on minorities were among the chief exhibits of those who attacked Prop 209 as a racist measure. Many predicted that over time blacks and Hispanics would virtually disappear from the UCLA campus.

And there was indeed a post-209 drop in minority enrollment as preferences were phased out. Although it was smaller and more short-lived than anticipated, it was still quite substantial: a 50 percent drop in black freshman enrollment and a 25 percent drop for Hispanics. These drops precipitated ongoing protests by students and continual hand-wringing by administrators, and when, in 2006, there was a particularly low yield of black freshmen, the campus was roiled with agitation, so much so that the university reinstituted covert, illegal racial preferences.

Throughout these crises, university administrators constantly fed agitation against the preference ban by emphasizing the drop in undergraduate minority admissions. Never did the university point out one overwhelming fact: *The total number of black and Hispanic students receiving bachelor's degrees were the same for the five classes after Prop 209 as for the five classes before.*

How was this possible? First, the ban on preferences produced better-matched students at UCLA, students who were more likely to graduate. The black four-year graduation rate at UCLA doubled from the early 1990s to the years after Prop 209.

Second, strong black and Hispanic students accepted UCLA offers of admission at much higher rates after the preferences ban went into effect; their choices seem to suggest that they were eager to attend a school where the stigma of a preference could not be attached to them. This mitigated the drop in enrollment.

The quest for racial sensitivity has created environments in which it is not only difficult but downright risky for students and professors, not to mention administrators, to talk about what affirmative action has become.

Third, many minority students who would have been admitted to UCLA with weak qualifications before Prop 209 were admitted to less elite schools instead; those who proved their academic mettle were able to transfer up to UCLA and graduate there.

Thus, Prop 209 changed the minority experience at UCLA from one of frequent failure to much more consistent success. The school granted as many bachelor degrees to minority students as it did before Prop 209 while admitting many fewer and thus dramatically reducing failure and drop-out rates. It was able, in other words, to greatly reduce mismatch.

University Officials Ignore the Need for Reform

But university officials were unable or unwilling to advertise this fact. They regularly issued statements suggesting that Prop 209's consequences had caused unalloyed harm to minorities, and they suppressed data on actual student performance. The university never confronted the mismatch problem, and rather than engage in a candid discussion of the true costs and benefits of a ban on preferences, it engineered secret policies to violate Prop 209's requirement that admissions be colorblind.

The odd dynamics behind UCLA's official behavior exist throughout the contemporary academic world. The quest for racial sensitivity has created environments in which it is not only difficult but downright risky for students and professors, not to mention administrators, to talk about what affirmative action has become and about the nature and effects of large admissions preferences. Simply acknowledging the fact that large preferences exist can trigger accusations that one is insulting or stigmatizing minority groups; suggesting that these preferences have counterproductive effects can lead to the immediate inference that one wants to eliminate or cut back efforts to help minority students.

The desire to be sensitive has sealed off failing programs from the scrutiny and dialogue necessary for healthy progress. It has also made racial preferences a force for economic inequality: academically well-prepared working class and poor Asian and white students are routinely passed over in favor of black and Hispanic students who are more affluent as well as less well-prepared.

The way racial preferences affect student outcomes is only part of the story. Equally relevant is the way the academic community has proved unequal to the task of reform—showing great resourcefulness in blocking access to information, enforcing homogenous preference policies across institutions, and evading even legal restrictions on the use of preferences. All of this makes the quest for workable reforms—which are most likely to come from the Supreme Court—both more complex and more interesting than one might at first suspect.

Academic Institutions Should Not Lower Their Standards for Minorities

Sarah Siskind

Sarah Siskind is a student at Harvard University where she is a columnist on The Harvard Crimson.

The Supreme Court is in the midst of hearing a suit against the University of Texas at Austin by Abigail Fisher [decided on June 24, 2013]. She maintains she was the victim of an admissions process that elevates skin color above academic qualifications and gives unfair advantage to minorities.

Academic Institutions Should Have Equal Admissions Standards

But who counts as a "minority" in affirmative action? Unfortunately for Ms. Fisher, adorable gingers are not considered a minority (despite red hair occurring in only 1–2 percent of the world population). So clearly, not just any minority can qualify as a "minority."

Perhaps affirmative action is meant to help those who have historically been discriminated against. It would be hard to overlook women and Jews when considering historical punching bags. However, women and Jews are indeed overlooked in the affirmative action policies of most schools.

Perhaps affirmative action attempts to help those groups heavily correlated with lower incomes. One of the strongest correlations with lower incomes is held by those with lower centers of gravity. As if short people didn't have it bad enough:

Sarah Siskind, "Affirmative Dissatisfaction: Affirmative Action Does More Harm than Good," *The Harvard Crimson*, November 2, 2012. Copyright © 2012 by The Harvard Crimson. All rights reserved. Reproduced by permission.

being refused at roller coasters, being unable to stand in the shallow end of pools, and now, being denied affirmative action. At least they don't have to stand in the back for pictures.

Finally, what about intellect? Perhaps our universities are in dire need of diversity of intelligence. Counter to most stereotypes, ugliness is highly correlated with poor intellectual performance by traditional measures, though I don't know how many qualified applicants will be willing to put that down on their application.

Race-based affirmative action attempts to target these groups: the discriminated against, the poor, and those with unique experiences and intellectual merits. However, affirmative action is fundamentally flawed because it uses race instead of targeting these groups themselves. Less academically qualified applicants should be treated as such, unless they come from poorer households and therefore do not have access to the same amount of resources as other applicants. However, this would be class-based affirmative action, not race-based.

Helping those with primarily low academic qualifications into primarily academic institutions makes as much sense as helping the visually impaired become pilots. How would you feel if you were assured before going into surgery that your surgeon was the beneficiary of affirmative action in medical school? I do not see why higher academic institutions should lower their standards for admission.

Affirmative action imbeds racism in the lives of future generations.

Discriminating on the Basis of Race Is Still Discrimination

In a way, I am the product of a sort of affirmative action, and it takes a terrible psychological toll. My father went to Harvard College, which makes me a legacy. I am kept up at night by the thought that simply because my father has attended and donated to the University, I might have taken the spot of a more qualified applicant. My name is not exactly "Sarah Wigglesworth Hurlbut Coop," but I am still a legacy, and the thought of its bearing on my admission is somewhat terrifying.

This is not a partisan issue. Many Democrats have, in confidence, heartily agreed with my position. Michael Bloomberg, mayor of New York City, has flatly denied proposals for affirmative action in the competitive application process for elite public high schools: "You pass the test, you get the highest score, you get into the school—no matter what your ethnicity, no matter what your economic background is." Supreme Court Chief Justice [John] Roberts stated it succinctly in a decision concerning affirmative action: "The way to stop discrimination on the basis of race is to stop discriminating on the basis of race."

The libertarian in me gags at the thought of infringing a private institution's selection criteria, but the aspiring lawyer in me points to the Fourteenth Amendment, which prohibits race-based discrimination. This amendment has since been somewhat modified with the 2003 Supreme Court case upholding the University of Michigan's use of affirmative action, *Grutter v. Bollinger*. In sum, the status of affirmative action has been in something of a legal flux. In the current case of *Fisher v. University of Texas*, Supreme Court Justice Elena Kagan recused herself, so a tie is possible, which would favor the defendant and uphold the status quo of legal affirmative action.

Even if affirmative action rights the injustices of widespread discrimination, as proponents allege, what about the beneficiaries down the line? As Supreme Justice Clarence Thomas argued, employers will likely regard a minority candidate with greater skepticism if their alma mater engaged in affirmative action. This wouldn't be racism—it would be simple logic—and that is what makes it all the more nefarious. I'm not saying racism doesn't exist. Racism persists, despite over a century of incredible progress, but affirmative action imbeds racism in the lives of future generations.

Racial Considerations Are Arbitrary and Unconstitutional

Carl Cohen

Carl Cohen is a professor of philosophy at the University of Michigan.

Abigail Fisher, a white applicant to the University of Texas, contends that the university, in giving preference to minority applicants while rejecting her, discriminated against her unlawfully because of her color. The Supreme Court will hear the case this fall [2012]; it is likely that Fisher will prevail. The Texas 10 percent law and the special circumstances of that university present complications, of course, but the makeup of the Supreme Court today differs importantly from that of the Court that decided *Grutter v. Bollinger* in 2003, which authorized universities to use race in admissions in some circumstances.

Racial Preferences Are Unconstitutional

But how will Fisher prevail? Put another way, how much of *Grutter* will remain standing when this decision comes down? Might *Grutter* be flatly overturned? Many fervently hope for that, and I am among them. *Grutter v. Bollinger* is one of those decisions that were wrong on the day they were decided; it is the *Plessy* [*Plessy v. Ferguson* upheld the separate but equal doctrine] case of the 21st century. *Fisher v. University of Texas* is a fine vehicle with which the Court may put *Grutter* into the dustbin of history, where in any case it is very likely to go before long.

In support of Fisher, 17 and one half amicus briefs have been put before the Supreme Court. Every one of them is powerfully argued and penetrating in its way. Without pretending to do full justice to each of those briefs, I here offer as fair and balanced a review of them as I am able, given the unavoidable use of categories and summaries.

First, a number of the briefs call for the outright reversal of *Grutter v. Bollinger*. The Texas Association of Scholars puts this best, perhaps, when it says forthrightly: 'Racial preferences of any type, and irrespective of the motivation for their use, are unconstitutional under all circumstances.' That wise spirit is echoed repeatedly, and in every case defended eloquently: 'Racial categories are arbitrary and ultimately incoherent' (American Center for Law and Justice); 'The Equal Protection Clause prohibits classifications of individuals based on race except in the rarest of circumstances,' and therefore 'a governmental racial classification is presumptively invalid and may be upheld only upon a showing of extraordinary justification' (Mountain States Legal Foundation); 'Race and ethnically-based admissions policies are crude, inherently ambiguous, and unsound constructs that can never be narrowly tailored to further a compelling interest in diversity' (Judicial Watch and Allied Educational Foundation); 'The use of race-conscious policies in pursuit of a non-remedial interest, like the interest in "diversity" approved in *Grutter v. Bollinger*, violates the principle of equal opportunity for military personnel' (Allen B. West, member of Congress and lieutenant colonel, U.S. Army, ret.). Summing it all up quite pithily is the statement of the American Civil Rights Union, 'The time has come to end racial preferences in college admissions.'

Second, it is entirely possible, perhaps even probable, that the Court will find for Fisher on narrower grounds. In *Grutter* it was made plain that universities ought to rely upon race-neutral alternatives if they can by so doing achieve the appropriate objective. Texas had enacted a law ensuring admission to the University of Texas to the top 10 percent of every high school graduating class in Texas, and had achieved thereby a degree of racial diversity at UT greater than that achieved earlier using preferences. That settles the matter without overturning *Grutter*, according to a brief submitted by the group Current and Former Federal Civil Rights Officials: 'The legislature's 10 percent plan was an effective race-neutral alternative.'

The University of Texas has not sustained, and cannot sustain, its burden of proof.

Racial Preferences Harm Other Minorities

Third, other minorities, Asian Americans and Indian Americans especially, are seriously discriminated against by the preferences used at the University of Texas. Their voices are raised very effectively in some of the amicus briefs submitted. The Asian American Legal Foundation and the Judicial Education Project write: 'Racial diversity programs discriminate against Asian-American individuals by treating them as members of an overrepresented and hence disfavored race'; and, moreover, 'Discrimination against Asian-American individuals in order to benefit other races is odious and demeaning to individual students.' Yes, odious and demeaning is just what it is. A group of five organizations including the National Federation of Indian American Associations, the Indian American Forum for Political Education, and the Global Organization of People of Indian Origin contends that race is frequently 'a decisive factor in college admissions, most greatly disadvantaging fully qualified Asian American students.' This group, joined by the Louis D. Brandeis Center for Human Rights Under Law, presents and defends the painfully telling point that 'The pretexts employed to limit Asian American School Enrollment are indistinguishable from those utilized to impose quotas against Jews throughout much of the past century.' Touche!

Fourth, the University of Michigan hornswoggled the Supreme Court in 2003 by insisting that its law school never used numbers or percentages in preferring minorities, but was seeking nothing more than 'a critical mass' of minority students. It was a clever and successful dodge. Chief Justice William Rehnquist, in his *Grutter* dissent, examined the numbers closely and demonstrated, with a clarity that ought to have embarrassed my university, that this position was an outright 'sham.' Now in the amicus briefs in *Fisher* the 'critical mass' theory gets a solid drubbing. Twenty-two distinguished scholars of economics and statistics from many universities join in one brief arguing that empirical evidence simply does not demonstrate 'that minority students are benefited by a "critical mass" of minorities in the classroom.' Indeed, they conclude, 'No reliable empirical evidence known to [these] amici supports the critical mass theory.'

They go on to present, in a detailed appendix, sets of comparisons of the performance of blacks and whites in classrooms of different sizes with different numbers of each. The 'critical mass' theory is statistically demolished. The theoretical demolition is provided by the Mountain States Legal Foundation, reaching this conclusion: '"Critical mass," like societal discrimination, is an amorphous and indefinable concept that cannot be addressed by a narrowly tailored remedy.'

There Is No Proof of the Benefits of Diversity

Fifth, one of the most infuriating aspects of the *Grutter* decision was the way in which the Court deferred to the University of Michigan, accepting its account of its needs without good evidence. Again in *Fisher* the Fifth U.S. Circuit Court of Appeals accepted the mere declaration of the University of Texas of its need for classroom diversity to achieve its educational mission. But, as the Southeastern Legal Foundation points out, the Supreme Court has previously been consistent in applying the 'strong basis in evidence' test where racial classifications have been employed, and 'Institutions of higher education are not immune from the obligation to show a strong basis in evidence,' which Texas surely has not done. The Cato Institute, in its brief, gives this argument powerful support, showing that 'The concerns motivating the strong-basis-in-evidence requirement apply with special force to universities' use of racial classifications to achieve diversity. . . . A university must demonstrate by a "strong basis in evidence" that its use of racial classifications is necessary to achieve a compelling interest.' No such basis in evidence has been provided. The University of Texas has not sustained, and cannot sustain, its burden of proof.

The previously supposed merits of diversity are illusory, without foundation.

The history of university conduct in this sphere underscores this requirement, and this point is made with quiet drama by the brief of the Center for Individual Rights [CIR], the group that carried (along with the Maslon law firm in Minneapolis) the years-long burden of the Michigan cases. The CIR points out that the Supreme Court's current 'narrow tailoring' jurisprudence 'encourages stealth.' Universities behave deviously, advancing their objectives (in the words of Justice Ruth Bader Ginsburg) with 'winks, nods, and disguises.' Their declarations are not to be trusted, certainly ought not be deferred to. 'Experience with racial preference by universities,' contends the Center for Individual Rights—which has had more such experience than any other organization—'further militates in favor of a searching strict scrutiny.' Yes it does; and such scrutiny was almost entirely absent in *Grutter* as also in *Fisher*.

The ugly history of racial discrimination in higher education is examined perceptively in the brief of the California Association of Scholars (joined by the Center for Constitutional Jurisprudence, the Reason Foundation, the Individual Rights Foundation, and the American Civil Rights Foundation). That history, they point out, renders higher education 'an unlikely recipient of the Court's deference on issues of race.' This brief also explores the very special circumstances under which the uses of race may be found rightly 'compelling'—circumstances certainly not realized in the *Fisher* case.

Sixth, the most powerful of all the amicus briefs are those that marshal the evidence—copious, detailed, and reliable evidence—that simply cuts the ground from under the *Grutter* decision. That decision was based entirely on the Court's belief that diversity was a central and absolutely compelling need for the University of Michigan and for all universities. Diversity, that decision concluded, was not simply a good thing, but a thing so absolutely necessary that even the temporary abandonment of the Equal Protection Clause of the Fourteenth Amendment must be allowed in order to achieve it. But this is hogwash. The Court in *Grutter* was bamboozled. Several of the current amicus briefs point that out with cool ferocity.

The brief of Abigail Thernstrom, Stephan Thernstrom, Althea Nagai, and Russell Nieli is nothing short of dynamite. With a careful review of the evidence presented by distinguished, reliable, and impartial social scientists, they prove how incredibly mistaken the premise of that argument was. They examine all that is known about diversity and its impact, and they conclude, without reservation, that the previously supposed merits of diversity are illusory, without foundation. They show that in fact we can now be confident that diversity has consequences almost the reverse of those the Court had supposed. Their quiet language belies the explosive impact of their findings. 'The primary justifications for the use of race-based preferences in higher educations admissions that the Court relied on in *Grutter* are flawed and fail to support the notion that there is a compelling state interest in diversity in higher education.' They go on to demonstrate the truth of a claim that I have myself been defending for years, on the basis of long experience at the University of Michigan: 'The mere fact that racial diversity increases contact between students of different races does not improve race relations among students.' That's right; it does not.

Racial Preferences Harm the Intended Beneficiaries

An unusual but very informative brief has been submitted by Richard Sander and Stuart Taylor Jr.—in support of neither party! Hence I report that the number of briefs in Abigail Fisher's support is 17 and one half. But this half is important. Sander reports: 'Social science research has undermined the central assumption underlying all racial preference programs in higher education admissions: that they are good for the intended beneficiaries.'

The costs attendant to racial classification outweigh any benefits that flow from a diverse student body.

Rick Sander is my friend, a fine statistician as well as a professor of law at UCLA. He long ago published an influential essay in which he demonstrated statistically that minority students who, by dint of preference, enroll in law schools to which they would not otherwise have been accepted suffer markedly as a result. They do less well in school, and they prosper less in their subsequent professional lives, than would have been the case had they attended schools for which they were indeed qualified. The artificial mismatch created by affirmative action results in lower class rankings, inferior professional appointments, and substantial injury to their careers.

This theme is defended in detail in his amicus brief: 'Key assumptions accepted by the Court below are doubtful: Evidence suggests that large racial preferences add little classroom diversity and do not make the university more attractive to minority candidates.'

An allied and penetrating explanation of some of the negative consequences of race-preferential admission is presented by three members of the U.S. Commission on Civil Rights: Gail Heriot (my personal heroine), Peter Kirsanow, and Todd Gaziano. They marshal scientific evidence showing that race-preferential admissions, although 'intended to facilitate the entry of minorities into higher education and eventually into high-prestige careers,' do the opposite. Such preferences 'have the effect of discouraging preference beneficiaries from pursuing science and engineering careers, . . . discouraging minority students from becoming college professors, . . . [and] decreasing the number of minority students who graduate and pass the bar.'

Finally, there is the one brief that is most persuasive overall, that of the Pacific Legal Foundation, the American Civil Rights Institute, the National Association of Scholars, and the Center for Equal Opportunity, whose president, Roger Clegg, is the most penetrating, knowledgeable, and tenacious of all current opponents of race preferences. This brief argues, along with the Thernstroms and others, that 'the benefits that flow from a diverse student body are highly dubious.' But more than all the others, this brief underscores the negatives, explaining with care and depth why 'the costs attendant to racial classification outweigh any benefits that flow from a diverse student body. Government racial classifications are destructive of democratic society; government racial classifications dehumanize us as individuals; racial preferences in college admissions cause serious harm to the very students the preferences are intended to benefit.' No rational person can read this eloquent set of arguments thoughtfully and continue to suppose that racial preferences for the sake of diversity are a good thing. They are poison.

The Pacific Legal Foundation, the ACRI, the NAS, and the Center for Equal Opportunity conclude, appropriately, by explaining why the principles of stare decisis, worthy of great respect of course, 'do not support the preservation of the highly flawed Grutter decision.'

Racial Preferences Do More Harm than Good

These, then, are the principal arguments of the amicus briefs. I will be forgiven, I trust, if I formulate two arguments that are implicit throughout and that deserve explicit emphasis.

Even if one grants arguendo . . . that there really are substantial merits flowing from diversity in an entering university class, the many undeniable negative consequences inherent in racial categorizing must be weighed against them.

First, racial classifications are appraised by the federal courts with 'strict scrutiny.' Under this high standard, a racial classification, if it is to be permitted, must be 'necessary to further a compelling governmental interest.' When does a state interest become 'compelling'? The concept of a compelling interest deserves reflection.

There may be occasions on which a state is obliged to use racial classifications because, in the light of the racially discriminatory history within some institution, there is no other way in which to give appropriate recompense for the racial injuries earlier done. In such circumstances the use of race may indeed be compelling, because if the state is to do justice, as it is morally obliged to do, there is no alternative. It is that recognition of unavoidable moral obligation that brings the concept of compulsion into this arena.

With this clearer view of the concept of a 'compelling state interest,' we can see that a program that offers educational advantages, even if those are substantial advantages, cannot be compelling in the moral sense. There may be rare exceptions in extraordinary circumstances, but the state's use of racial classification, departing from the Equal Protection Clause, can in general be justified only by some moral compulsion. This explains why the justifiable uses of race have almost invariably been in remedial circumstances, righting identifiable wrongs. It also helps to explain why using racial categories to avert supposed dangers (as when Japanese-American citizens were ordered into internment camps during World War II) is so deeply offensive.

Second, even if one grants arguendo [for the sake of argument] (as I surely do not grant in fact) that there really are substantial merits flowing from diversity in an entering university class, the many undeniable negative consequences inherent in racial categorizing must be weighed against them, as the brief of the Pacific Legal Foundation, et al., makes clear. After that weighing, it is only the residual balance of the two that can serve as a defense of the diversity rationale. Because those negative consequences are in fact grave, the residuum on the side of the diversity rationale is certainly slight, if there is any residuum at all. And it is that residuum of advantage (if any) that must be accepted as compelling if the rationale is to succeed. It is (in sum) the results all things considered that must be compelling for that diversity rationale to be persuasive. Yet that outcome, on balance, is probably negative.

If there are any residual advantages of diversity all things considered (which in my view is not the case), they cannot be morally compelling. The diversity rationale must therefore fail even if the weighing of advantages and disadvantages were to result in a positive outcome for diversity. To call diversity 'compelling' in the context of state action is a category mistake. *Fisher v. University of Texas* gives the United States Supreme Court an opportunity to correct this unfortunate error.

CHAPTER 2

Should Colleges Consider Legacies in the Admissions Process?

Overview: Legacy Students Have a Significant Advantage in College Admissions

Elyse Ashburn

Elyse Ashburn is director of communications at the University of Maryland Baltimore County.

Family connections help you get into college. And a new paper suggests that at highly selective colleges, they may count even more than was previously thought.

Legacy Status Counts for a Great Deal

A researcher at Harvard University recently examined the impact of legacy status at 30 highly selective colleges and concluded that, all other things being equal, legacy applicants got a 23.3-percentage-point increase in their probability of admission. If the applicants' connection was a parent who attended the college as an undergraduate, a "primary legacy," the increase was 45.1-percentage points.

In other words, if a nonlegacy applicant faced a 15-percent chance of admission, an identical applicant who was a primary legacy would have a 60-percent chance of getting in.

The new study is sure to add fuel to the debate over the role of legacy admissions, particularly in determining who gets into the country's most-sought-after colleges. And it sheds light on advantages that colleges themselves may not have even been fully aware of. The author, Michael Hurwitz, controlled for a broader range of variables, such as student character and high-school activities, than had traditional analyses.

In doing so, he found that the other, more-common method underestimates the advantage for legacies.

"Some colleges may think this admissions advantage is justifiable or they may use the findings to reshape their policies," says Mr. Hurwitz, a doctoral candidate in quantitative policy analysis at the Harvard Graduate School of Education.

He also looked at the difference between legacies with a primary connection and those with looser connections—a parent who attended graduate school, or a sibling, grandparent, aunt, or uncle who attended as a graduate or undergraduate. He found that the tighter connection, while less common, provides a much larger benefit.

"The takeaway to me is that here's a study that seeks to control for a number of factors and finds that legacy status is even more important than previously thought," says Richard D. Kahlenberg, a senior fellow at the Century Foundation and the editor of *Affirmative Action for the Rich: Legacy Preferences in College Admissions*. "It's more evidence that this is not a feather on the scale."

For an individual applicant, legacy or nonlegacy status may indeed matter a lot. But Mr. Hurwitz cautions that because of the size of the applicant pools at the sample colleges, legacy admits don't greatly decrease other students' already-long odds of acceptance. Of the 290,000-plus applications he studied, only about 6 percent had legacy status.

Traditional Studies Underestimated Legacy Advantage

An article on his study, "The Impact of Legacy Status on Undergraduate Admissions at Elite Colleges and Universities," was published last month [December 2010] in the journal *Economics of Education Review*. The data come from 133,236 unique applicants for freshman admission in the fall of 2007 at 30 highly selective private colleges and universities.

Mr. Hurwitz's research found that legacy students, on average, had slightly higher SAT scores than nonlegacies. But he was able to control for that factor, as well as athlete status, gender, race, and many less-quantifiable characteristics. He also controlled for differences in the selectivity of the colleges.

Across the board, primary legacies got a greater advantage than secondary legacies.

He was able to do so by focusing on the large number of high-school students (47 percent) who submitted applications to more than one of the colleges in the sample. A given applicant's characteristics, like the wealth of their family or strength of their high school, wouldn't vary from college to college. But their legacy status would, and so too might their admissions outcomes. (Mr. Hurwitz also ran an analysis that showed that students who applied to multiple colleges were representative of the overall pool.)

He found that traditional analyses, which control for some of the major quantifiable measures, like SAT scores, but for fewer variables overall, underestimated the legacy advantage. What that means, he says, is that some unquantifiable aspects of legacies' applications—such as life experiences, type of high school, or extracurricular activities—must otherwise work against their chances of admission. But he says, "the data aren't rich enough to tell what that is."

Thomas J. Espenshade, a professor of sociology at Princeton University who has done key research on legacies, says that the new estimates are not widely different from those in previous studies, but that, nonetheless, the larger advantage is notable. Previous studies also had not looked at differences between various familial connections, he says.

A Handed-Down Benefit

Across the board, primary legacies got a greater advantage than secondary legacies. The difference seemed to matter the most at the most-selective colleges in the sample, those with an average base acceptance rate of just under 10 percent. Secondary legacy status at those top-tier colleges conferred an estimated advantage of 8.7 percentage points, while primary legacy gave a 51.6-point advantage.

Legacy status of any kind mattered more at the most-selective and least-selective colleges than it did at those in the middle tiers. The data didn't reveal why, but Mr. Hurwitz thinks that, because such a small proportion of qualified applicants are admitted at the most-selective colleges, any edge over another applicant is magnified—while the less-selective colleges may be most eager to cultivate alumni loyalty and giving.

The data set did not contain information on giving, so Mr. Hurwitz could not look at how much of the legacy advantage comes simply from having relatives who attended a college versus from having relatives who not only attended a college but also donated to it.

Mr. Hurwitz also looked at how students within certain SAT ranges fared against one another. There wasn't a clear-cut pattern, but generally the higher the SAT score, the more legacy status mattered. That finding, Mr. Hurwitz says, seems in line with colleges' argument that legacy status matters the most in deciding between two highly-qualified candidates. "It's easier to justify nudging the student if they're really strong academically," he says.

Richard H. Shaw, dean of undergraduate admission and financial aid at Stanford University, says his office considers students to be legacies only if one of their parents earned a degree from the university, with an emphasis on undergraduate degrees. Such status is taken into account among many factors, he said, but it certainly does not trump competitive expectations. Mr. Shaw said the university's legacy admits are generally stronger than the median of the admitted class, based on quantitative measures, like test scores, rigor, and grades.

"Stanford also has a high percentage of admitted and enrolling first-generation students each year whose parents did not graduate from a four-year college or university," Mr. Shaw wrote in an e-mail. "We consider access and opportunity a very important principal. We also value intergenerational connections to the Stanford experience."

Several other highly selective colleges declined to comment or did not respond to requests for comment. Mr. Hurwitz will not name the colleges in his sample; he signed an agreement pledging not to do so in exchange for what would otherwise be private data.

Very few colleges, however, have admissions rates approaching anything as low as 10 percent. The study also references other research that has relied on similar data from a group called the Consortium on financing Higher Education, which comprises all the Ivy League institutions and two dozen other highly competitive private universities and liberal-arts colleges.

Whatever their identity, the colleges in the study are very selective. And Mr. Hurwitz says the findings are most likely to be of relevance to officials and would-be students at similarly-competitive colleges.

Legacy Students Help to Create a Sense of Community

Danielle Telson

At the time this viewpoint was written, Danielle Telson was a student at George Washington University and a reporter for the student newspaper, The GW Hatchet.

Calling on his experiences as University president, President Emeritus Stephen Joel Trachtenberg said he supports higher education admission policies that give a boost to children of alumni during a panel Wednesday [September 22, 2010].

Legacy Students Enrich Campus Life

The focus of the panel's discussion was a new book [*Affirmative Action for the Rich: Legacy Preferences in College Admissions* by Richard D. Kahlenberg] concerning the downfalls and moral ramifications of legacy preferences in higher education institutions. Members of the panel included three co-authors of the book arguing the unfairness of legacy preference.

While other panel members argued the unconstitutionality of favoring the children of university alumni, Trachtenberg said he sees advantages to admitting the children of dedicated alumni.

"The single most important benefit of having gone to Harvard or Yale is that you had an education and you could in some way pass one of the benefits of this education onto your children," Trachtenberg said.

He said admitting the children of an alumnus to an institution of higher education had little to no bearing on a class or a university as a whole. He said he regards legacy preference as a community building technique in universities.

Trachtenberg gave an example of how GW admissions counselors select the incoming freshman class, having to choose from 20,000 applicants a class of only 2,000.

"The goal is to choose a group of people that actually want to be there, and a group that will get along with each other. If you choose only the most qualified, you could end up with a class of 2,000 girls who will be very disappointed when looking around on the first day of freshman year," Trachtenberg said.

Trachtenberg argued that by using legacy as a part of the application, the class of students ends up being a group from all backgrounds and that desire to be at the school.

He said legacy preference also gives families the sense that they belong to a community. He referenced GW's discount on tuition as a way of contributing to this idea. With this policy, if a student comes to GW while their sibling is already enrolled, they can receive a discount of 50 percent off tuition.

"We want to encourage families to think of George Washington as their university," he said of why the policy began.

Panel member Steve Shadowen, an attorney specializing in commercial litigation and a law professor, said that 86 percent of the top 200 ranked universities in the nation use legacy preference, thus "shutting the door on the children of college dropouts or low-income parents."

During the question-and-answer period of the luncheon, Trachtenberg countered this point by saying that these students may not get into a top-choice school, but that they will also find a school they can belong to.

While he said he supports legacy preference, Trachtenberg acknowledged that there are limits to legacy admissions. He said that if 30 percent of an admitted class was legacy, that would definitely raise moral issues.

In response to an audience question about what the admission situation would be if legacy preferences were abolished at all schools, Trachtenberg said nothing would change.

"Many legacy students would get into top-ranking schools even without the legacy advantage," he said.

Stop Worrying About Legacy Admissions

Daniel Luzer

Daniel Luzer is the web editor of the Washington Monthly *and writes the magazine's higher education blog, the* College Guide.

Legacy preferences: the blight of the academic institutions of the Republic! That dammed practice of letting people in based on who their parents are. That elitism is shameful and un-American. Why are we still doing this?

So wonder many progressives, in a more or less annual rant that comes around at admissions time. According to an editorial in *The New Republic*:

> The country's most selective schools continue the deeply unfair practice of favoring legacies in their admissions process. According to journalist Daniel Golden, 33.9 percent of legacy applicants to the University of Pennsylvania were admitted in 2008, compared with just 16.4 percent of the overall pool. The numbers are even more dramatic elsewhere: At Princeton, in 2009, 41.7 percent of legacies were admitted, compared with 9.2 percent of overall applicants. What sort of institution devoted to meritocracy more than quadruples its admission rate for the children of the well-connected?

What sort of institution? Well this isn't much of a mystery: it's an institution that relies on significant private funding. It makes sense for colleges to admit the relatives and children of alumni. That's because if they don't admit them the alumni might get mad and stop giving money.

But even if it's practical, it does sound a little odd. America is one of the only places in the world where a parent's alma mater has any bearing whether a student can be admitted to the university of his choice.

And with all the focus on test scores and grades, the college admissions process seems like a merit based slotting system, rewarding the most talented and assigning the untalented, or lazy, to America's less selective schools. America seems to have no problem with that basic method of operation, believing as it does that the process essentially rewards people for doing a good job and working hard.

Even admissions preferences for athletes, which occasionally come under fire from pundits, is not terribly troublesome. Being a good basketball or field hockey player probably isn't relevant to one's academic career, but at least it's a talent.

And then there are legacy preferences, the tendency of colleges to reward people for their genealogy. But is it *really* unfair?

Legacy preferences don't make America dumber or poorer, or even more unequal.

If the practice is unjust, it seems to be so only in a very limited, and irrelevant "I'm mad because I didn't get into Dartmouth" sense. The problem with the basic "down with legacies" argument is that it implies that the legacy preferences of selective colleges prevent otherwise deserving people from getting a great education. This is wrong; if someone doesn't get into his top school only because he's not a legacy he won't be hurt; he will get into one of the other selective schools to which he applied.

The fact that a high school student didn't get into Princeton or Dartmouth despite straight A's, perfect SAT's, and impressive extracurricular activities is unfortunate, for sure, but it doesn't matter. Such a student probably will get into Cornell or Williams, and almost certainly will be admitted to George Washington or BU. And all of those schools are pretty much the same, in terms of the demographics of the students who go there and the types of jobs they hold and lifestyles they lead once they graduate.

Legacy preferences don't make America dumber or poorer, or even more unequal.

There are so many applicants to America's top schools that if Princeton eliminated legacy preferences it would merely admit more affluent, bright students whose parents didn't go to Princeton. Removing legacy preferences wouldn't actually put more poor students in; the number of low-income students otherwise capable of being admitted to selective schools is pretty limited.

Elite colleges often talk about the nature of meritocracy, how important it is for wealthy, selective schools to make it possible for students to succeed there. It's important to hold schools to this pledge, but let's keep this in perspective.

As the Supreme Court determined in Dartmouth College v. Woodward, the private American college does not exist for some ambiguous public improvement project; it exists to do as its trustees see fit. Part of the reason these schools can afford to be so generous is because they have devoted, generous alumni willing to give to make their school great. There's no evidence that any college will enroll legacy students who aren't otherwise prepared to succeed to college, but colleges have to keep the wishes of its generous graduates in mind.

That means the institutions can give out scholarships and build new buildings, it also means keeping alumni happy. An easy, and cheap, way to do this is to give legacy preferences. As long as no one gets hurt (and no one really does) the preference for such applicants makes a lot of sense. It's time to let this one go.

Legacy Students Explore Campus Life Through Historic Lens

Hannah Loewentheil

Hannah Loewentheil is a student at Brown University and a staff writer for the campus paper, the Brown Daily Herald.

For some students, initial interactions with the University aren't when they receive the fat letter in the mail, but through the photos in their parents' old yearbooks or college anecdotes passed down through the generations.

Legacy students are those with at least one close relative—a parent, sibling or grandparent—who attended Brown. Though legacy admissions have become controversial in recent years, students at Brown with alum relatives face the same challenges of finding a place within Brown's community. What distinguishes them is a family history tied to the University and a unique connection with its past.

Keeping It in the Family

Bryn Coughlan '14, daughter of James Coughlan '84, always had her heart set on Brown, she said.

"Brown was everything I wanted, and I idolized it since I was a kid," Coughlan said.

Growing up, she was well-acquainted with the Brown campus and attended summer lacrosse clinics offered annually by the women's lacrosse team. She followed in the footsteps of her father, a member of the men's lacrosse team, by joining the women's squad her freshman year. Coughlan's younger brother, Jimmy, will be a member of Brown's class of 2017 and will also play varsity lacrosse.

But Coughlan said she and her brother were not pressured to apply. On the contrary, "my father didn't want me to come here, not because he didn't like Brown, but he didn't want me to base my decision around the fact he went here," Coughlan said.

Coughlan called herself "narrow-minded" during the application process, an attitude that her father dissuaded. She conducted a varied college search, considering both New England Small College Athletics Conference schools and some larger universities. Once Coughlan's father understood his daughter had seriously considered her options, he supported her decision to apply to Brown, she said. At the end of the day, "nothing compared to the unique environment at Brown," she added.

Michael Kader '14 had a very different experience. "I mostly thought that I wouldn't get in, and so I didn't want to apply," Kader said. His mother, Kim Kader '84, strongly urged him to apply to Brown and Duke, where she attended medical school. Kader was accepted to multiple selective schools, but ultimately decided on Brown. "I came to ADOCH and fell in love with the people and the atmosphere," he said.

Kader said he has followed in his mother's footsteps more than he anticipated, deciding to concentrate in neuroscience just as she did. Though he originally planned to concentrate in bioengineering, he fell in love with neuroscience after taking a class during his first semester. While his mother played women's volleyball her freshman year, Kader also has become involved in athletics, devoting most of his extracurricular time to the club tennis team.

Kader's younger brother, Jonathan, is a member of Princeton's class of 2014, breaking with family tradition. Jonathan said he hoped to be recruited to play tennis and centered his college search around athletics, though he ulti-mately changed his mind about participating.

"If I was sure then that I didn't want to play tennis, I probably would've applied early to Brown," he said. "I thought it would help me to apply because of my legacy there," he added.

Jonathan was admitted to Brown among other universities, and he decided on Princeton. He said his decision was diffi-cult. "I think both my mother and my brother wanted me to go to Brown," he said.

William Van Deren '15 said his father, John Van Deren '80 MD '83, influenced his decision to apply to Brown.

"My father would tell me stories about Brown, and I was definitely influenced by it because from a young age I heard what a wonderful school it was," Van Deren said.

But Van Deren's decision to apply to Brown was ultimately his own.

"My father never tried to divert me away from other schools," he said.

Attending Brown has done more than strengthen the family's ties with the University. "I think coming here has cre-ated a new bond with my father," Van Deren added. He said he is able to tell his father stories about Brown, knowing that he had similar experiences and could relate.

A Controversial Practice

Given admissions are becoming more selective by the year, legacy status has become a controversial issue.

Most admissions officers say legacy status is only enacted as a tie-breaker.

The University admitted only 9.6 percent of overall appli-cants to the class of 2016, and other Ivy League institutions were equally, if not more, selective that year, *The Herald* reported. Harvard admitted only 5.9 percent of applicants, followed by Yale at 6.8 percent and Columbia at 7.4 percent.

According to an article in the *Chronicle of Higher Education,* about 10 to 25 percent of students at selective colleges and universities are legacies. Statistics from the *New York Times* reveal that 33 percent of applicants offered admission to Princeton's class of 2015 were legacies. According to the article, "Harvard generally admits 30 percent, and Yale says it admits 20 percent to 25 percent."

Opponents to legacy admission say the concept perpetuates the traditional white, Anglo-Saxon, Protestant Ivy League demographic. The *Chronicle* cited polls in 2010 that revealed 75 percent of Americans that responded reject legacy preference in admissions. Instead, opponents advocate inclusive programs like affirmative action initiatives and the expansion of need-blind financial aid.

But most admissions officers say legacy status is only enacted as a tie-breaker. In situations where two applicants are equally qualified, legacy status only provides a slight edge.

Many institutions prefer to maintain family ties. Though opponents to legacy admissions say an attending family member may encourage alums to donate, proponents argue college admissions are decided on individual characteristics rather than familial coffers.

Passing It On

Despite her legacy status, Coughlan said she has never doubted she belongs at Brown.

"I understand that legacy puts me in a different pile in the admissions process," she said. "But I deserve to be here, and I think that the majority of other students recognize that too," she said.

Kader said he does not usually bring up the fact his mother attended Brown unless asked. "I don't think there is that much of a stigma that if your parents went here you don't deserve to be here," he said.

"I openly tell people that my dad went here," Van Deren said, noting that the community has always been accepting. "I always felt qualified to get in on my own."

Coughlan said though Brown "fits exactly what I want," she wants her children to decide the college they attend on their own.

"I want my kids to be able to get in here on their own so they have the option of getting in anywhere they want," she said.

Colleges' Elitist Legacy Preference

Scott Stern

Scott Stern is a student at Yale University where he is a guest columnist for the Yale Daily News.

At the end of this academic year, Yale's Dean of Undergraduate Admissions, Jeffrey Brenzel, will return to the classroom. As the college ushers a new face into the admissions office, it's time to initiate a new era for admissions practices by eliminating a policy conceived in elitism, dedicated to the proposition that not all applicants are created equal. At Yale and beyond, institutions of higher education would benefit from eliminating the unfair practice of legacy preference.

There are many motivations that drive the policy of giving advantage to applicants whose parents or family members are alumni. Legacy applicants continue a loyal family tradition, legacy preference is an effective tiebreaker in admissions, it's assumed that legacy applicants come from intellectually rich and educationally prepared backgrounds, and legacy preference ensures that schools remain closely connected with alumni, who may reciprocate generously.

Giving preference to legacy applicants, however, has its roots in the troublesome historic practice of trying to propagate a white educational elite. Richard Kahlenberg, a senior fellow at the Century Foundation and editor of *Affirmative Action for the Rich: Legacy Preferences in College Admissions*, explains that "legacy preferences began after World War I, part of an effort to curtail the enrollment of immigrant students, particularly Jews, at Ivy League colleges." He goes on to note that legacies are still disproportionately white, citing findings that "underrepresented minorities make up 12.5 percent of the applicant pool at selective colleges and universities but only 6.7 percent of the legacy-applicant pool." "This racial disparity," he concludes, "is likely to continue for legacies in the next generation."

At Yale, having alumni family members is no insignificant asset. According to Dean Brenzel, the college treats "legacy status as a positive factor in the evaluation process, and in recent years legacies have been admitted at about three times the rate of non-legacies." He cautions, however, that "the degree of advantage does not correspond to the difference in admit rates, because legacy applicants on average present academic qualifications substantially stronger than non-legacy applicants. In other words, the average legacy applicant is more competitive in the process, even without any regard paid to legacy status."

The question is then: If the children of alumni are, on average, "more competitive" to begin with, why do they need an extra boost?

The children of those who attended elite colleges are likely to have advantages distinct from those whose parents were not so lucky.

Out of 1,351 students who entered Yale in 2011, 182 had parents who attended Yale for undergraduate or graduate school. That's 13.5 percent of the incoming class, an astonishing figure when you consider that if you met seven random freshmen at Yale last year, chances are one of their parents attended the institution. This is more than a preference given to break ties; it's blatant nepotism.

Many institutions contend that all students benefit from the resources secured through legacy preference, which potentially fund financial aid to low-income students, staff salaries, or new facilities. Accepting the children of alumni at higher rates might be seen as an unspoken quid pro quo—we'll take your kids, you'll buy us a new chem lab. Yet this logic is flawed. Yale's legacy policy prioritizes the school's financial interests over its stated mission to find "exceptionally promising students of all backgrounds." When questioned about the percentage of legacy students who identified as students of color or the percentage of legacy students on financial aid, Yale's admissions office replied: "we don't track or publish these kind of subgroup statistics." A 1991 study at the comparable institution Harvard does shed some light, finding that legacy advantage disappeared almost entirely when a legacy applicant inquired about financial aid.

While exceptions exist, it's fair to claim that the children of those who attended elite colleges are likely to have advantages distinct from those whose parents were not so lucky. Coming from a home that, on average, is wealthier and emphasizes education is no small advantage. The single greatest correlating factor in whether you will attend college is whether your parent attended college. This is the ultimate unfairness of legacy preference: Even if it is only used as a tiebreaker, it breaks the tie in the wrong direction. Non-legacy kids are more likely than legacy kids to have succeeded in the face of obstacles, but in a theoretical "tie" with a legacy applicant, selective schools take the legacy.

As Yale's administrators decide on a direction for the office of admissions, they should consider ending a practice that elevates those already advantaged in a misguided attempt to secure donations. When Yale gives an unneeded advantage to students of a certain background—mostly wealthy, mostly white—it detracts from its mission. Legacy preference not only negatively affects non-legacy students, it has a detrimental effect on Yale by reducing the diversity of backgrounds among its students that the university claims to support and cherish.

The Price of Admission

Gillian Tett

Gillian Tett, a columnist and editor at the Financial Times, *is also the author of* Fool's Gold: How Unrestrained Greed Corrupted a Dream, Shattered Global Markets and Unleashed a Catastrophe.

Almost three decades ago, I applied to Cambridge university in England for an undergraduate degree. Just before my interview, a schoolteacher proffered some advice: "Don't mention that your father went to Cambridge—or not unless you are asked!"

The reason? Back then in 1980s Britain, there was an aversion to the idea that family connections could help students get an elite university place. Indeed, the only thing considered more taboo by admissions officers was the idea that somebody could "buy" their way into a university with charitable donations, coupled with family ties.

How times change. Or, more accurately, how perceptions vary according to geography and social customs. This autumn, the children of several American friends entered a clutch of elite US colleges, such as Brown, Harvard and Princeton. Most of these kids have earned their places, in the sense of having high-performing SAT tests and a curriculum vitae packed with accolades. And yet these intelligent teenagers had another advantage: connections. More specifically, their parents and relatives are usually alumni of those elite universities, visibly involved in the alumni network and have often made philanthropic donations.

To be sure, those parents usually do not want to stress this aspect of their kids' lives: it would be rude to ever discuss the "price" of securing a spot (ie, how much philanthropy or alumni involvement is required). But there is no shame incurred by the practice either. On the contrary, when I relate my Cambridge tale it provokes astonishment. This is little wonder, perhaps, when educational researchers estimate that at 15 per cent or more of students at some top Ivy League universities are "legacy" kids—and having a family link increases a mid-level student's chance of entry by about 60 per cent.

"It is just how the system works," says a friend in Washington, a prominent Harvard alumnus who proudly helped get his nephew to Harvard this year. "My nephew is incredibly bright—he deserves to be there. But the problem is that there are lots of other bright kids, so I did everything I could." Or as Lawrence Summers, former Harvard University president, has observed, "legacy admissions are integral to the kind of community that any private educational institution is"—or they are in the eyes of Ivy League leaders and some private liberal arts colleges.

The legacy system contributes to bifurcation in the education world.

Don't get me wrong: in telling this story I am emphatically not suggesting that Britain's educational system is a paragon of effectiveness or meritocracy. There is hypocrisy aplenty in those British norms. With or without legacies, most students at Oxford or Cambridge come from privileged backgrounds. And there is a practical problem too: precisely because institutions such as Cambridge will not sell places for philanthropy, they are cash-strapped compared with the likes of Harvard.

But while the American cultural standards are arguably more honest—and far more commercially effective—they carry potentially debilitating consequences. And what I find truly striking is just how little this system is openly discussed, particularly compared to the whole issue of positive discrimination (or the idea of awarding places proactively on the basis of race, say, which has sparked a storm of discussion in America in recent days). One problem of the legacy system is that it entrenches privilege. It also gives the student body of the Ivy League a bifurcated, if not caste feel. For while a commendably large chunk of students at Ivy League schools study on scholarships, there are relatively few children from "middle" families—those too wealthy to qualify for aid but not wealthy and elite enough to pull strings.

More damaging still, the legacy system contributes to bifurcation in the education world. These days, many private Ivy League institutions are drowning in funds because of those alumni donations. Indeed, fundraising is usually cited as a key benefit of that legacy system. But while Harvard, say, has plenty of largesse, much of America's publicly funded higher education system is being crushed.

Over in California, for example, the public universities that cluster around Berkeley are currently facing "draconian" cuts, as Nathan Brostrom, executive vice-president, says. Indeed, they have already lost a third of their state aid in the past five years.

But it is tough for Berkeley to replace that state money since the colleges do not practise a legacy policy at all: instead, Brostrom says that 40 per cent of students come from low-income families (compared with 10 percent at Ivy League institutions).

And the State University of New York, which runs a vast network of public community colleges and universities, has had "its state tax support reduced by $1.4bn, or 30 per cent" in the past four years, says Nancy Zimpher, its chancellor. That cuts the New York state share of SUNY's budget from 34.1 per cent to 26.9 per cent. Zimpher is working with the state to create more stability, and is trying to replace this with private money. But that "is tough", since SUNY has no legacy policy and no real tradition of raising private funds. After all, hedge fund managers are unlikely to give millions to a community college to secure a place for their children. Their largesse typically either goes to their alma mater or to fund a school for poor, photogenic, little kids.

This is a tragedy. After all, what happens (or does not happen) at a place such as SUNY is crucial for future American growth. Or to put it another way, if America is going to stay competitive and cohesive, it desperately needs to create decent higher education for a wide swath of its population— and not just for an elite that is becoming adept at reproducing privilege across generations, under the banner of donations.

Legacy Students Are Already Advantaged and Do Not Need Additional Help

Shikha Dalmia

Shikha Dalmia is a senior analyst at the Reason Foundation. The following article has been edited for publication in this book.

College-bound high school students do not always lose their chastity before graduation, but they certainly lose their innocence. Nearly every senior who has gone through the admissions mill can recount stories of peers with outstanding academic records—class valedictorians with stellar SATs and perfect GPAs [grade point averages]—who were passed over by top colleges while others with far more modest credentials got the nod. *The New York Times* reports that Harvard turned down 1,100 applicants with perfect 800s on the math SAT this year. Yale rejected several with perfect 2400s on the three-part SAT exam. Princeton said no to thousands with 4.0 GPAs.

College Admissions Practices Are Arbitrary

To many frustrated parents, one word describes the admissions process at America's elite universities: arbitrary. But that's not the word admissions officials use, as I discovered two summers ago when I toured a dozen or so East Coast campuses with my son, a high school junior at the time. Asked what kind of grades and scores made kids competitive for their schools, officials in university after university insisted, as if reading off the same memo, that the review process was "holistic," "comprehensive," or "individualized." Grades, we were repeatedly told, "are only one among many factors we consider."

Another such factor is race. Nearly every selective college, public and private, gives a sizable edge to underrepresented minorities. Before the U.S. Supreme Court outlawed the University of Michigan's undergraduate admissions criteria in *Gratz v. Bollinger* (2003), the school relied on a complicated rating system that awarded points for several personal and academic factors, including skin color. Black and Hispanic candidates automatically got 20 points. A great essay counted for only one point; a perfect SAT score, a mere 12.

But as Justice Clarence Thomas observed in his dissent in a companion case, race is not the only factor that distorts college admission decisions. "The entire [college admission] process is poisoned by numerous exceptions to 'merit,'" he noted.

The Wall Street Journal's Daniel Golden exposes those other exceptions in his 2006 book *The Price of Admission*. Golden shows that elite schools routinely hand preferences to athletes; to the children of faculty, celebrities, and politicians; to "development cases" whose fabulously wealthy parents offer hefty donations up front; and, above all, to the offspring of alumni. Universities expect the parents of these "legacy" candidates to contribute to their coffers after their children are admitted.

Legacy preferences are the original sin of admissions, the policy that fundamentally compromises fair, merit-based standards.

Robert Birgeneau, chancellor of the University of California at Berkeley, told Golden that at one Ivy League school only 40 percent of the seats are open to candidates competing on pure educational merit. According to a 2005 study by the Princeton sociologists Tom Espenshade and Chang Y. Chung,

in 1997 nearly two-thirds of all these non-race-based preferences at elite universities benefited whites, even though whites
comprised less than half of all applicants that year.

We have a vigorous national movement to eradicate racial
or minority preferences, at least in public universities. In 2006
Michigan became the third state in the country after California and Washington to approve a ballot measure imposing a
constitutional ban on the use of race in admissions at state-
run schools and in government hiring decisions. And this year
[2008] the author of all those bans—Ward Connerly, a black
California businessman—is stepping up his crusade. He has
launched petition drives in Oklahoma, Missouri, Colorado,
Nebraska, and Arizona to put similar measures before voters
in November.

But there's no comparable effort to get rid of legacy preferences. Even more troubling, many prominent opponents of
racial preferences greet suggestions to get rid of legacies, the
mother of all preferences, with a perfunctory nod—or a gap-
ing yawn.

It shouldn't be that way. Legacy preferences are the original sin of admissions, the policy that fundamentally compromises fair, merit-based standards. Universities can't in good
conscience tip the admission scales for the more privileged
and then ask the less privileged to compete solely on merit.
What's more, eliminating race while keeping legacies will make
the admissions process less fair, not more fair, because it will
open up minority slots to competition by whites but not vice
versa.

Legacy preferences are an especially terrible idea for tax-
supported public universities, since they make it possible for
rich, white, and less qualified kids to take seats that are at least
in part supported by the tax dollars of poor, minority families. Private schools, of course, should be free to admit whom-
ever they want, and it is therefore tempting to ignore their use
of legacies. But there are few genuinely private schools in

America anymore, thanks to the enormous amount of federal funding they accept. And setting public policy aside: Just as a matter of propriety, should there be room for legacies at institutions that market themselves as bastions of meritocracy? The use of legacies by the Harvards, Yales, and Princetons of the world dilutes the standards of excellence they pretend not merely to uphold, but to embody. . . .

A Small Problem?

Legacy preferences, like racial preferences, are repugnant because they reward not individual virtue or accomplishment, but an accident of birth that has no relevance for a college education. Moreover, just because they aren't linked with an egregious history of racial abuse does not justify turning a blind eye to them. India has a far uglier record of discrimination by caste than race. Yet no one would argue that it ought therefore to concentrate only on eradicating caste discrimination and treat race as a non-issue.

Even seemingly small differences in scores translate into significantly higher rates of acceptance for legacies over "unhooked" candidates.

It is true that the use of legacies is mainly limited to undergraduate programs in the more selective public and private schools. Racial preferences, on the other hand, pervade every aspect of every school—from undergraduate and graduate admissions to faculty hiring and promotion. Moreover, according to a 2007 paper by Princeton's Douglas S. Massey and Margarita Mooney of data from 28 elite universities, while 77 percent of minorities had standardized test scores below the institutional average, about 48 percent of legacies did. In rare exceptions, such as Middlebury College, legacies actually scored higher than the institutional average.

How far below average do those legacies and minorities score? It's impossible to get up-to-date, nationwide data on the subject, given the universities' secrecy, but the late psychologist Richard Herrnstein and the social scientist Charles Murray reported one telling piece of information in their 1994 book *The Bell Curve.* In 1990, the average student admitted to Harvard scored 697 on the verbal SAT and 718 on the math section. By comparison, legacies scored 674 on verbal and 696 on math—a 47 point difference. Combined minority scores hover at about 100 to 150 points below the institutional average.

What's more, even when universities lower admission standards for legacies, they don't lower them as much as they do for minorities. As mentioned before, the Michigan point system used to award 20 bonus points to under-represented minorities—the equivalent of boosting a 3.0 GPA to a 4.0. By contrast, it handed only four points to children of alumni.

But such statistics don't tell the full story. Given how intense the competition is for the nation's most selective schools, even seemingly small differences in scores translate into significantly higher rates of acceptance for legacies over "unhooked" candidates—admissions lingo for those who don't qualify for any preferences.

According to the October 1996 *Brown Alumni Magazine,* 40 percent of legacy applicants were accepted to Brown University, as opposed to 19 percent of the total applicants. The Office of Civil Rights similarly found in 1990 that children of alumni were twice as likely to be accepted at Harvard over more qualified students who did not get legacy or athletic or any other preferences. And a study by the Center for Equal Opportunity, a Virginia-based think tank, found that at the University of Virginia, after controlling for test scores, grades, and other academic credentials, a legacy candidate had 4.3 times higher odds of admission than non-legacy applicants in 1999.

Universities claim that legacy status is never a major or decisive factor in their admission decisions. It's only used, they say, as a tie-breaker among otherwise comparable candidates. That's what they claimed about racial preferences too, and that turned out to be false. Indeed, it is hard to really know how much weight universities award to legacies given their stubborn refusal to reveal their admissions data or even talk about their admission policies. (University of Michigan officials, for instance, declined repeated requests to discuss this issue.) But why do legacies deserve any edge, big or small?

Racial preferences, at least originally, were meant to remedy discrimination—both historic and current—against blacks. What is the justification for favoring the offspring of Harvard, Yale, and Princeton alumni? Unlike many inner-city kids, they grow up in families with a strong pro-education ethos. They have access to the finest public or private high schools in the country. Their parents can spring for tutors, standardized test preparation courses, and even consultants to help them write essays and complete their college applications. "These are kids who grow up with every privilege," notes Connerly. "They don't deserve any additional advantage."

Legacy policies protect groups that are already in, at the expense of those that are trying to break in.

Moreover, though the policy of using legacy as a "tie-breaker" among equivalent candidates sounds innocuous, it has perverse consequences for one group in particular: Asian Americans. Asians don't benefit from racial preferences because they are not considered underrepresented minorities. And they don't benefit from legacy preferences because they tend to be the children of first-generation immigrants. Espenshade, the Princeton researcher, found that while legacy and athletic preferences offset the effects of racial preferences on whites, they compound them for Asian Americans. According to Espenshade's regression analysis of data from a dozen selective colleges, on a 1600-point SAT scale, being black and Hispanic adds up to an advantage of 230 and 185 extra SAT points respectively. The preference for legacies translates into an edge of 160 points. By contrast, being Asian American represents a 50 SAT-point disadvantage.

The CIR's [Center for Individual Rights Terry] Pell, however, argues that the legacy problem is "self-correcting." Racial preferences have become so ideologically embedded that universities will never abandon them unless forced to by courts or voters, Pell maintains. But as the ethnic mix of the broader population changes so does the composition of the student body. A generation later, then, so will the composition of the beneficiaries of legacy preferences.

But the problem with legacies is not that they never adjust to shifting demographics. It is that they slow the process of adjustment. Legacy policies protect groups that are already in, at the expense of those that are trying to break in.

Practical Benefits?

Conservatives pride themselves on being sensible realists, not starry-eyed utopians eager to stamp out every form of social injustice regardless of consequences. This tendency partially explains their squishiness on the legacy issue. On the one hand, they don't dispute that legacy admissions border on institutionalized nepotism—rewarding children for the accomplishments of their parents and relatives. On the other hand, enforcing a strict merit-based standard seems a tad fanatical given all the practical benefits of legacy policies for universities.

One purported benefit is that legacies are an important source of funding for universities. Not only do more legacies donate to universities, they donate in greater amounts. For instance, according to the *Cavalier Daily*, the University of

Virginia's student newspaper, 65 percent of legacy parents contributed to the university's 2006 capital campaign, compared with 41 percent of non-legacy parents. Moreover, legacy parents on average coughed up $34,759 each whereas non-legacy parents gave only $4,070.

It is far from clear that universities lack "legacy-neutral" tools to . . . "maximize their profits."

All in all, legacies alone account for over 30 percent of the private donations to most elite colleges. "If mild preferences to legacy students allow universities to maximize their income, is that so objectionable?" asks Thernstrom.

Without such donations, universities claim, they could not invest in high-quality faculty and facilities and remain competitive. Even more important from the standpoint of social justice, universities say they couldn't maintain need-blind admission policies. These policies allow colleges to admit students purely on academic grounds—and then offer financial aid to anyone unable to afford the roughly $50,000 per year it costs in tuition and living expenses to attend a top-notch university these days. Without legacy contributions, such aid would supposedly become more difficult, and elite campuses would truly become playgrounds of the rich.

But [Stephan] Thernstrom and Pell don't buy arguments from social utility when it comes to racial preferences. Like other conservatives, they insist that universities that want to help inner-city minorities need to find race-neutral ways that don't selectively dilute academic standards for some groups. Nor do they believe that the educational benefits of a diverse student body are real or big enough to justify giving minorities a leg up.

Yet they uncritically accept the business and social case for legacy preferences. And it is far from clear that universities lack "legacy-neutral" tools to—as Thernstrom puts it—"maximize their profits." They could conceivably rake in more money by auctioning off a certain number of freshmen seats every year to the highest bidders. But elite universities would never entertain a scheme like that, because it could cost them their "elite" reputations. It would expose precisely how much they are diluting their admission standards for how many and for how much. This kind of information would erode their aura of selectivity—the very thing that makes them attractive to legacies and everyone else.

Connerly, after spending years on the University of California board, is not convinced that alumni will stop contributing to their alma maters if their kids don't get preferential treatment. Indeed, as Golden noted in *The Price of Admission*, Caltech is able to tap alumni money without offering any edge to their children. For instance, Caltech in 2001 obtained a $600 million pledge—the largest gift in the history of higher education at the time—from Gordon Moore, cofounder of Intel, neither of whose two sons attends the university. Caltech's commitment to high standards and excellence is a core part of its sales pitch to raise money from alumni and non-alumni alike.

Golden offers other examples, albeit isolated ones, of schools that have built sizable endowments through business strategies that don't rely on legacy preferences. Cooper Union, a highly prestigious and selective art school in New York that offers a free education to everyone admitted, for decades lived off income generated through its investments in real estate. Berea College, a small college in Kentucky exclusively targeted toward low-income kids, has accumulated a startlingly large endowment by making its progressive credentials a selling point to potential donors: It is the South's first inter-racial, coeducational college and was founded by an abolitionist minister. Its mission is to educate and uplift impoverished Appalachian families.

Legacy money doesn't seem to boost the presence of low-income kids on elite campuses by subsidizing their educations, either. The schools that get the most legacy money—Harvard, Yale, and Princeton—are among the worst when it comes to the economic diversity of their students. In his 2005 book *The Chosen: The Hidden History of Admission and Exclusion at Harvard, Yale and Princeton*, Berkeley sociologist Jerome Karabel reported that among the top 40 schools, Princeton and Harvard are ranked at 38th and 39th, respectively, when it comes to such diversity, and Yale 25th.

If elite colleges were serious about offering equitable access to genuinely talented students, they could find business models that don't involve legacy preferences.

For a contrast, look at Caltech. It is the nation's most meritocratic private university that eschews all preferences, and it is among the 10 most economically diverse schools. Nor is it hard to understand why. Admissions are a zero-sum game with many candidates vying for a finite number of seats. The crucial determinant of economic diversity on campus therefore becomes not how much largesse legacies expend on poor kids but how many seats they take away from them.

If elite colleges were serious about offering equitable access to genuinely talented students, they could find business models that don't involve legacy preferences. If they have not done so, it is because the government won't—and market forces can't—hold them accountable.

Is There Any Rationale for Legacies at Public Schools?

The core mission of taxpayer-funded public universities is not to conduct research, promote economic growth, or correct broader social problems. It is to expand higher education opportunities. That, at any rate, is what the general public believes: Respondents in a 2003 survey conducted by *The Chronicle of Higher Education* overwhelmingly picked "offering a general education to undergraduates" as the top priority among 21 different roles that public universities could play.

Those who oppose race as a factor in admissions but ignore legacies open themselves to accusations of inconsistency and hypocrisy.

Taxpayers perceive different public universities as fulfilling this educational mission in different ways. They regard land-grant universities as catering to rural kids, urban universities to commuters who can't live on campus, community colleges to students not served by traditional four-year colleges. There is something problematic, even oxymoronic, about the very idea of "elite" public universities whose doors are by definition shut to the vast majority of taxpayers who fund them. If they must exist, they should exist to serve academically gifted kids. Thus the only defensible admission policy for these universities is one that allows all gifted kids an equal shot at admission.

This is precisely what legacy and other preferences don't allow. They reduce the fate of applicants to the discretion of admissions bureaucrats, eliminating clear-cut standards applied equally to all. Preferences replace the rule of law with the rule of men. . . .

Can Meritocracy Prevail?

America's fundamental promise is that individuals ought to control their destiny through hard work and talent, not arbitrary accidents of birth. Legacy preferences are no less damaging to this promise than racial preferences. Those who oppose race as a factor in admissions but ignore legacies open themselves to accusations of inconsistency and hypocrisy. But, worse, to the extent that they succeed in dismantling race while leaving legacies intact, they risk putting in place a less—not more—fair admissions system.

As their battle against racial preferences heats up this year, they need to open another front against legacy preferences. The U.S. Constitution and courts do not offer ready weapons for the new battle. But that hardly justifies laying down arms without a fight.

There are plenty of ways at the state level to stop the use of legacies at public universities, from constitutional bans to state mandates requiring more transparent admission policies. Government can't ban private universities from using preferences, legacy or racial or any other, without running afoul of the Constitution. But that doesn't mean that moral suasion can't be used to prod them toward fairer admissions policies. Public outrage recently forced Harvard to give up its early decision program. The program, which overwhelmingly benefited the rich and connected, effectively lowered the bar for students who applied early and promised to accept its admission offer.

Most of all, we need policies to strengthen market accountability. We need to end the cartel-like character of the higher education industry, where private universities can keep consumers in the dark about their admission practices and educational product and still charge exorbitant prices without worrying that a competitor will emerge to challenge their market dominance with a cheaper and better product. An honest and straightforward recognition of the dangers of legacy preferences will go a long way toward bringing about such reforms.

Legacy Preferences Discriminate Against Minorities

Kathryn Ladewski

Kathryn Ladewski is a government attorney. The opinions in the viewpoint are the author's and do not reflect the position of the United States government or its agencies.

Social mobility is one of the hallmarks of American society. The American Dream is one in which people of all backgrounds, with hard work and a little bit of luck, can be successful. One component of this "dream" is intergenerational social mobility and the idea that the opportunities of future generations are not limited by the past. Access to higher education is a key component of intergenerational social mobility, and historically it has been one way for vulnerable groups, such as immigrants and minorities, to achieve greater prosperity. Legacy preferences, which give an admissions "boost" to university applicants whose parents or grandparents attended a particular institution, run counter to intergenerational social mobility because they allow the composition of past generations of university students to influence the composition of future generations of students. In addition, legacy preferences disproportionately benefit white university applicants, whose parents are more likely to have attended American universities.

Legacy Admissions Discriminate Against Minorities

Legacy policies were first implemented in the 1920s as a mechanism for excluding Jewish students and other immi-

Kathryn Ladewski, "Preserving a Racial Hierarchy: A Legal Analysis of the Disparate Racial Impact of Legacy Preferences in University Admissions," *Michigan Law Review*, vol. 108, no. 4, January 2010, pp. 577–601. Copyright © 2010 by Kathryn Ladewski. All rights reserved. Reproduced by permission.

grants from university admission. Since that time, legacy policies have become widespread at public and private universities
across the United States. The justification for such legacy policies has changed over time—they are now intended to promote institutional loyalty and increase alumni volunteerism
and donation rates, rather than to disadvantage certain groups
of applicants. Despite this changing purpose, legacy policies
continue to have a negative effect on the admissions prospects
of immigrant and minority applicants, whose parents are less
likely to have attended college in the United States.

This [viewpoint] argues that legacy admissions policies are
impermissible under the Civil Rights Act of 1964, which prohibits universities receiving federal funds from promulgating
policies that have a racially disparate impact, unless those
policies actually promote a legitimate purpose. . . .

---

*The negative impact of legacy preferences on minority
applicants is based on past patterns of attendance at
American universities and the underrepresentation of
such racial groups over that period.*

The Racial Impact of Legacy Preferences

Although defenders of today's legacy preferences argue that
the preferences are needed for fundraising purposes and are
not intentionally discriminatory, such programs have a racially
discriminatory effect. . . . Because legacy policies improve admissions prospects for alumni children, the racial composition
of students admitted under legacy preferences is necessarily
affected by the racial composition of the previous generation
of college students. College students of previous generations
were less diverse than today's applicants, and legacy preferences allow those past enrollments to influence the current
generation of admits. Because legacy preferences benefit children of alumni, "[t]he racial and ethnic composition of the

pool of potential legacy students necessarily resembles the composition of past student generations."

The disparity between the racial composition of legacy applicants and the overall applicant pool is apparent today at both public and private universities that employ legacy preferences. For example, the United States Department of Education Office for Civil Rights determined that although Asian Americans made up 15.7% of overall applicants at Harvard between the years 1985 and 1992, Asian Americans represented only 3.5% of legacy applicants. Similarly, at the University of Virginia, where black students made up approximately 10% of entering students in 2002, only 3% of legacy applicants in that same year were black.

Such figures are perhaps unsurprising given that previous generations of American university students were overwhelmingly white, particularly at many universities that use legacy preferences. At the University of Virginia, for example, explicit segregation continued into the 1950s and fewer than 3% of students were minorities as late as 1973. At Harvard, each class year only included five or six black students until the 1960s. At the University of Pennsylvania, black students represented only 5.7% of undergraduates as late as 1996. Because previous generations of college students at these and other universities exhibited a relatively high degree of racial (white) homogeneity, admissions policies that benefit the children of alumni also tend to disproportionately benefit whites.

Because the negative impact of legacy preferences on minority applicants is based on past patterns of attendance at American universities and the underrepresentation of such racial groups over that period, the negative impact of legacy preferences on racial minorities should decrease over time if the student bodies at American universities continue to diversify. However, research suggests that it will be some time before the racial composition of legacy admits mirrors the racial composition of admitted students overall. At the University of

Virginia, for example, where black students made up 10–12% of the student population in the 2003–04 academic year, a statistical simulation predicted that black students would not make up a similar proportion of legacy admits until the year 2020.

Legacy preferences at Harvard help to explain why Asian American applicants in the early 1990s were admitted less frequently than their white peers despite having higher academic qualifications. In fact, after removing legacies and recruited athletes from the sample, the United States Department of Education Office for Civil Rights [OCR] determined that Asian Americans were actually admitted at a higher rate than whites for three of the ten years in the sample. In that study, OCR determined that Asian American applicants were admitted at a rate of approximately 4.2 percentage points less than white applicants (13.2% admit rate for Asian Americans versus 17.4% for whites). This statistically significant difference in admissions rates was fully explained by the comparatively low proportion of Asian Americans who were legacy applicants and recruited athletes, two groups that were (and are) given an advantage in Harvard's admissions process. The experience of Asian American applicants at Harvard demonstrates that the impact of legacy preferences is significant enough that it was readily apparent to applicants and community leaders.

Statistical Analysis of University Fundraising Data

Universities that employ legacy admissions policies generally justify them as assisting with university fundraising efforts. Despite these universities' assertions, however, statistical evidence calls into question whether legacy preferences actually benefit fundraising efforts. This Part presents the results of a statistical analysis of fundraising data from eight public universities, all of which have eliminated their legacy admissions policies. [These universities include six in the University of

California system (Berkeley, Davis, Irvine, Los Angeles, Santa Barbara, and San Diego), all of which eliminated legacy preferences in 1999, as well as the University of Georgia and Texas A&M University, both of which eliminated legacy preferences in 2003.] After analyzing fundraising data from these universities before and after legacy preferences were eliminated, this Part concludes that discontinuing legacy preferences did not harm fundraising outcomes at these universities. . . .

[The] eight universities have experienced increased alumni and private donations over time, although those patterns are less apparent in the number of alumni donors. This increase in donations appears to be present irrespective of the universities' use or elimination of legacy preferences. Similarly, the total number of alumni donors does not appear to be strongly affected by the presence or absence of legacy preferences. . . .

The statistical evidence . . . suggests that no positive link exists between legacy preferences and alumni fundraising.

Legacy Preferences and the Civil Rights Act of 1964

The Civil Rights Act of 1964 prohibits educational institutions that receive federal funds from engaging in practices with disparate racial effects unless those practices actually further a legitimate purpose. The courts employ a burden-shifting standard to determine whether a federally funded university has violated this prohibition. Under this standard, the plaintiff first bears the burden of showing that a facially neutral policy has a racially discriminatory effect. If the plaintiff meets this burden, the defendant then has the burden to prove a legitimate justification. If the defendant succeeds, the burden returns to the plaintiff to show either (1) that the defendant's stated reason is actually pretext for discrimination, or (2) that an equally effective alternative practice exists that would result in less racial disproportionality. This Part argues that legacy preferences at federally funded educational institutions support a claim of disparate impact discrimination and, thus, violate the Civil Rights Act of 1964, because they do not actually promote a legitimate purpose.

Universities employing legacy admissions policies argue that they would be able to meet their burden under the second prong of the burden-shifting standard on the theory that such policies are beneficial fundraising tools. Indeed, courts are generally deferential to universities in allowing them to structure admissions practices according to their educational mission. In an affirmative action case, for example, the court in *Farmer v. Ramsay* stated that "courts are ill-advised to serve as super-admissions committees, replacing schools' professional judgments with their own." Similarly, the U.S. Supreme Court has said that judges "may not override [a genuinely academic decision] unless it is such a substantial departure from accepted academic norms as to demonstrate that the person or committee responsible did not actually exercise professional judgment." In the legacy admissions context, one district court [in *Rosenstock v. the Bd. of Governors of the Univ. of N.C.*] gave a one-paragraph analysis of the issue, taking a highly deferential attitude toward the university:

> Plaintiff also attacks the policy of the University whereby children of out-of-state alumni are exempted from the stiffer academic requirements necessary for out-of-state admission. Again, since no suspect criteria or fundamental interests are involved, the State need only show a rational basis for the distinction. In unrebutted affidavits, defendants showed that the alumni provide monetary support for the University and that out-of-state alumni contribute close to one-half of the total given. To grant children of this latter group a preference then is a reasonable basis and is not constitutionally defective. Plaintiff's attack on this policy is, therefore, rejected.

In general, therefore, courts tend to defer to universities' policies and educational decisions. . . .

Although courts are generally deferential to universities in setting their own policies, such deference is inappropriate in the context of a Title VI claim where a prima facie [at first sight] case of disparate racial impact has been shown. Universities that receive federal funds are subject to Title VI's burden-shifting framework; the university's burden in the second stage requires it to present evidence showing the relationship between legacy preference and a legitimate goal. Indeed, the defendant's burden in Title VI discriminatory impact cases is heavy. . . . In order to meet their burden, universities must produce evidence demonstrating a relationship between legacy policies and fundraising (or another legitimate goal). . . .

Because legacy preferences generate a disparate racial impact without any demonstrated benefit for a legitimate university goal, legacy preferences at federally funded universities represent impermissible disparate impact discrimination under the Civil Rights Act of 1964.

The statistical evidence . . . indicates that the relationship between university fundraising and legacy admissions policies does lend itself to statistical analysis and suggests that no positive link exists between legacy preferences and alumni fundraising. This statistical evidence suggests that, under the Title VI disparate impact framework, universities employing legacy policies would be unable to meet their burden of proof that legacy policies actually promote fundraising goals. Therefore, because legacy preferences have a disparate racial impact and they have not been shown to further any legitimate university objective, such preferences are impermissible under the Civil Rights Act of 1964.

Legacy preferences are a common component of university admissions programs that give a boost to applicants whose parents or grandparents attended a particular institution. Such preferences have a negative impact on minority and immigrant applicants, whose parents often did not attend college in the United States. This effect motivated the nation's first legacy preferences, which were implemented at Yale in the 1920s to limit the number of Jewish students.

Universities that employ legacy preferences often justify those preferences by arguing that they improve fundraising outcomes. But the statistical analysis presented in this Note suggests that legacy preferences do not positively impact university fundraising. Because legacy preferences generate a disparate racial impact without any demonstrated benefit for a legitimate university goal, legacy preferences at federally funded universities represent impermissible disparate impact discrimination under the Civil Rights Act of 1964.

CHAPTER 3

Should Athletes Get Preferential Treatment in College Admissions?

Chapter Preface

University of North Carolina learning specialist Mary Willingham was shocked to learn that several student athletes assigned to her for help with their homework could neither read nor write. Her experiences with athletes led Willingham to research the reading levels of 183 University of North Carolina at Chapel Hill (UNC) athletes who played football or baseball from 2004 to 2012. According to CNN reporter Sara Ganim, in "CNN Analysis: Some College Athletes Play Like Adults, Read Like 5th-Graders," Willingham found that 60 percent of the UNC athletes read between fourth- and eighth-grade levels and between 8 percent and 10 percent read below a third-grade level.

Following up on Willingham's research, CNN collected data on the SAT and ACT entrance exam scores of athletes playing football and basketball, considered revenue sports for the university. After reviewing the data, CNN concluded that between 7 and 18 percent of the revenue sport athletes were reading at an elementary school level, reported Ganim. The student athletes also scored significantly below their peers on SAT and ACT exams. While the national average for the SAT is 500, many student athletes scored in the 200s and 300s on the SAT critical reading test. The national average for the ACT is 20. However, the reading score for most student athletes in the CNN study was in the high teens.

These studies are consistent with data collected by the National Collegiate Athletic Association (NCAA), the organization responsible for administering college athletics. A 2011 NCAA survey revealed that the SAT scores for athletes are about 200 points lower than those for nonathletes. Additionally, the NCAA reports that the graduation rate for college football players is 16 percent lower than the college average and the graduation rate for college basketball players 2 percent lower.

Despite the evidence that student athletes are often less academically qualified than their peers, by other measures they excel, argues Ben Atlas in a 2012 article in *The Oracle*:

> The notion that sports-oriented students are "dumb jocks" is one of inaccuracy. The graduation rate of student athletes is 63 percent, one percent higher than average students. The National Collegiate Athletics Association (NCAA) projects graduation to rise in the coming years to 77 percent. African-American student athletes have a 10 percent higher rate of graduation than their non-athlete counterparts. In 2004, the NCAA studied a group of student athletes for ten years after high school. Within that time, 91 percent of the group were employed and 88 percent had some sort of degree.[1]

The debate over college admissions standards for athletes continues against the backdrop of public opinion, which is overwhelmingly weighted against preference given to athletes. In a 2013 Rasmusssen Reports national telephone survey, 71 percent of those surveyed believe that athletes should not get preferential treatment in college admissions compared to only 17 percent in favor, and the remaining undecided.

In the following chapter, educators, commentators, and journalists debate the issues concerning preferential college admissions treatment for athletes.

---

1. Ben Atlas, "Admissions Requirements for Athletes Should Remain Lenient," *The Oracle*, October 26, 2012. http://gunnoracle.com/2012/10/admissions-requirements-for-athletes-should-remain-lenient.

Athletic Recruitment Can Help Overall Enrollment

Libby Sander

Libby Sander is a senior reporter at The Chronicle of Higher Education.

For decades, the 40-acre meadow separating Adrian College from a state highway was an afterthought on the modest campus of low-slung limestone buildings.

But in less than three years, the grassy expanse, like the college itself, has undergone a transformation. The newly developed acreage—boasting an ice arena, football and baseball stadiums, a track, and a dozen tennis courts—is the cornerstone of a plan to raise enrollment through intense athletics recruiting.

And to the relief of college leaders concerned about the future of the small, private liberal-arts college, the plan appears to be succeeding more quickly than they had anticipated.

Since 2005, enrollment has surged 57 percent, to 1,470 students, the highest number in at least two decades. More than half of those students play varsity sports. The college has also become more selective: Three years ago, Adrian accepted 93 percent of the 1,200 students who applied. This year it accepted 72 percent of its 4,200 applicants. Faculty members, pleased with the trend, say the caliber of students in their classrooms has improved.

Administrators are optimistic that athletics recruiting will be a lasting antidote to the sinking enrollment and moribund student life that had plagued the institution. Coaches have quotas they must hit or lose their jobs. And the tuition dollars that athletes bring have already enabled the college to make much-needed improvements in academic buildings and to hire more faculty members.

"I have all the sports I need every time I turn on the television," says Jeffrey R. Docking, Adrian's president and a chief architect of the plan. "I would not have started one of these sports if I didn't think it was good for enrollment and the future of the college."

The use of athletics to drive enrollment, he says, could well be "the fountain of youth for small liberal-arts colleges."

Ready for Change

Adrian did have a head start. For years the college had owned but never developed the 40-acre meadow adjacent to the main campus. And when Mr. Docking arrived in 2005, the institution was in good fiscal health, with little debt, enabling it to more easily borrow large sums.

Persuading cash-strapped students to consider Adrian depended on offering something they couldn't get elsewhere. . . . That "something" turned out to be extracurricular activities—in particular, sports.

But problems abounded, and the Board of Trustees was ready to try something drastic. Enrollment had sunk to 935, well below the capacity of 1,400 students, and showed no signs of rising. Three residence halls were shuttered, the ones that remained open were falling apart, and retention rates were suffering.

In Michigan, a state with the highest unemployment rate in the nation, the college's total price tag of $24,800—which has since increased to $31,000—was hardly a recruiting advantage. Among Adrian's competitors are the state's many large, public institutions. Many of its students also apply to

Michigan State, Central Michigan, Western Michigan, and Wayne State Universities, says Carolyn Quinlan, director of admissions at the college for the past 24 years.

Persuading cash-strapped students to consider Adrian depended on offering something they couldn't get elsewhere, Mr. Docking says. That "something" turned out to be extracurricular activities—in particular, sports.

At the time, though, the college's athletics department was a modest operation, with only five full-time coaches. Recruiting had little oversight. Several of the teams, including the football team, competed on local high-school fields because the college lacked adequate competition space.

So, shortly after Mr. Docking took office, he and Richard A. Creehan, executive vice president, came up with a plan to present to the governing board. They called for an outlay of $30-million—roughly half of it borrowed and half of it raised from donors—to expand the athletics program and build sports facilities on the undeveloped land.

The idea, Mr. Creehan recalls, was: "Spend money to make money."

Rapid Expansion

In three years, in addition to building the new facilities, Adrian has added five varsity teams and six club teams. It has hired 11 new full-time head coaches. The plan requires the 16 head coaches of varsity sports to bring in a total of nearly 200 athletes each year.

"We say to these coaches, 'You have one job: Recruit,'" Mr. Docking says. "We've had to let go of coaches who haven't made their numbers." (The staff members who supervise the student newspaper, student government, cheerleading and dance teams, and marching band are also required to collectively recruit an additional 40 or so students annually.)

Several coaches, many of whom are in their 20s and have joined the college in the past two or three years, say meeting the numbers is well within their reach.

"It's a plan that works for people who love their job and want to be successful," says Chris Delfausse, head coach of the men's lacrosse team, which won eight of 14 games in its inaugural season last spring. The administration, he says, hires only coaches "who are attuned to what their message is and what their goals are, so it works out."

Money helps, too. The athletics department's operating budget has more than doubled since 2005, from $300,000 to $800,000. And recruiting expenses have grown even more significantly. In the 2006–7 academic year, Adrian spent $31,000 on recruiting, compared with $2,800 in 2001–2, according to the U.S. Department of Education.

Nearly half of this year's incoming class of 581—the largest in Adrian's 149-year history—is composed of varsity athletes.

The decision to include ice hockey and lacrosse among the new programs was strategic, as both sports tend to be popular in affluent areas. Also, in the Great Lakes states and Canada, hockey is among the most popular of sports, but in Michigan, only one other institution in the National Collegiate Athletic Association's Division III fields a hockey team.

And lacrosse is rooted in the mid-Atlantic states and New England, regions from which Adrian hopes to pull more students in coming years. It is also fast becoming one of the most popular sports at the high-school level in many suburban areas, including those near Detroit and Ann Arbor. But before the creation of men's and women's lacrosse teams at Adrian, Michigan had no Division III lacrosse programs. "Because we're the only program in the state, we're getting all the kids," says Mr. Creehan.

Athletes are now one of the largest groups on the campus. Last month the 300 or so athletes who returned for preseason workouts far outnumbered the entire freshman class from just three years ago. And nearly half of this year's incoming class of 581—the largest in Adrian's 149-year history—is composed of varsity athletes.

"They love the game, they love the sport, and they want to continue to play," says Mr. Creehan. "What we're saying is, 'You can continue to do that here.'"

"All I Could See Was Dirt"

For a college where only 22 percent of students hail from out of state, the task of spreading Adrian's name throughout the Midwest, let alone farther afield, is slow going.

"It's a step-by-step process," says Mr. Delfausse, the men's lacrosse coach. As he prepares to start recruiting his third class of players this year, he says he finally feels as though Adrian has enough name recognition to give him traction hundreds of miles away.

"In the first year, I don't think I called a kid in Maryland or New York or Massachusetts," he says. "Now we're actively going after more of the Maryland kids. It's still a long shot, but more kids are listening."

Ron Fogarty, coach of the men's hockey team, was given free rein to travel wherever he felt necessary. He recruited all but three of his 25 players last year from the junior hockey leagues that are popular in the upper Midwest, New England, and Canada. Half of the squad is Canadian; outside the ice rink, the Canadian flag flies next to those of the United States and Michigan.

One of the players Mr. Fogarty recruited was Adam Krug, of Livonia, Mich., a senior who is captain of the team and last year led Division III colleges in scoring. After competing in various junior hockey leagues after high school, Mr. Krug played two seasons for Wayne State, a Division I team.

When Mr. Fogarty suggested that Mr. Krug transfer to Adrian to play hockey, it was hardly ideal timing for a recruiting pitch.

"When I came on my visit, all I could see was dirt," says Mr. Krug, who at 25 has earned the nickname "Dad" from his teammates. "So you have to use your imagination."

The additional revenue from higher enrollment has enabled Adrian to make significant improvements in academic buildings and in faculty hiring.

Coaches and administrators at other institutions were skeptical of the philosophy of using athletics to increase enrollment, says Mr. Fogarty, whose team won 26 of 29 games in its inaugural season last year. "But now that they see it, they believe it," he says.

The additional revenue from higher enrollment has enabled Adrian to make significant improvements in academic buildings and in faculty hiring. As its operating budget has grown to $43-million from $23-million since 2005, the college has modernized two academic buildings, expanded the campus dining hall, and hired 16 tenure-track faculty members.

"It's exciting, and we're getting good stuff and better digs," says Beth M. Myers, a professor of English who serves as the college's faculty-athletics representative in NCAA matters. An alumna who has taught at Adrian for 28 years, Ms. Myers says she has seen various efforts to boost enrollment come and go. But the plan offered by Mr. Docking and Mr. Creehan "is the only one that's worked that's brought us a good group of students."

Few faculty members express reservations about the student population having so many athletes, Ms. Myers says. "We think athletes are a pretty good cross section of humanity. They have all the various backgrounds and issues and strengths that any group of students would have."

A New Look

A philosophy is useful in galvanizing coaches to recruit aggressively. But having brand-new facilities certainly helps to close the deal.

Visitors to the athletics complex at Adrian College walk on concrete sidewalks that are free of stains. Trees barely stretch above six or seven feet, and a drive on the unpaved access road to the most distant fields kicks up clouds of dust. A statue of a bulldog, the college's mascot, even sports a jersey with a large '06' on the back.

As the facilities rose from the meadow, they built momentum in the recruiting effort.

Natalie Niblock, 20, a junior from White Pigeon, Mich., transferred to Adrian last year from nearby Madonna University. Her older brother Troy, a senior at Adrian, is the starting quarterback and co-captain of the football team.

"I used to actually make fun of Adrian when he first came here his freshman year, because it looked way different," says Ms. Niblock. "I was like, 'Ew, yuck, it's so little.'"

Today she is happy with her decision to transfer. The opportunity to play volleyball was a crucial factor, she says, just as it was for many of her teammates. "We're all like, 'It's so expensive,'" she says. "If we didn't play volleyball, we wouldn't come here."

Still, Mr. Delfausse, the men's lacrosse coach, says he and other coaches would like to see the athlete population decrease slightly. "The majority of us would like to . . . have more of the student base be music or theater or the academic side of things," he says. "I think the school wants it that way as well in the long run.

"If you go too far to one side," he says, "you lose the balance."

Athletes Enrich a College Community with Their Diverse Backgrounds and Mindsets

The Daily Princetonian

The Daily Princetonian *is the student newspaper at Princeton University.*

While Jack Turnage's article, "When colleges recruit athletes, everybody loses," circulated around various social media feeds earlier this month, I felt it spoke directly to me. Though I was not one of Princeton's Olympians, I am a rising sophomore on the men's water polo team, and I can give you a clear picture of what it means to be a Princeton athlete and say why athletic recruiting is a beneficial part of the admissions process.

Being an Athlete Is Time-Consuming

Let me first dispel the notion that recruited athletes are so-called "dumb jocks" undeserving of their education. When understanding the demands on an athlete, others often forget the rigors of practice, competition and travel. During the season, being on the water polo team takes up at least 20 hours a week, not to mention the added time spent dealing with the related mental and physical fatigue. Schedules are even more rigorous at schools outside of the Ivy League. Thus, if collegiate athletes do in fact perform lower than their peers, we have to take into account that athletes have significantly more commitments than the average student.

Even with the disadvantage of having less time, athletes often still find a way to do just as well as their peers if not even better. For instance, my roommate, running back Chuck Dibilio, earned Ivy League Rookie of the Year honors last season. After each game, he would literally change, eat, and then immediately start working on his weekly economics problem set. He worked tremendously hard and did very well academically.

I saw Chuck's story countless other times, and at other schools as well. Growing up in Palo Alto, Calif., I saw how Stanford athletes balanced world-class academics with world-class athletics. Andrew Luck graduated with honors as an architectural engineering major. Oh yeah, he was a decent football player too.

In terms of admission, perhaps athletes might get by with a lower academic record, but this is designed to acknowledge that playing sports at a high enough level to be recruited will detract from time spent doing homework and studying for tests. I'm sure most students would agree that time is a huge factor in raising grade point average or your SAT score.

Perhaps a school might need to lower its academic standards to bring in these great athletes, but for everything that they bring to the table, I am absolutely convinced that it is the right thing to do.

Athletes Bring Diversity to a Campus

The goal of the admissions office isn't to make a class consisting entirely of 4.0-GPA, 2400-SAT academic superstars. Rather, the goal is to grant every undergraduate an enriching college experience. Athletes offer something different to a school community—they bring a different background and mindset while having unique strengths and interests. Collegiate competitions bring school communities together, uniting and inspiring students of all backgrounds.

My favorite story is the one of swimmer Scott Weltz, a University of California, Davis alumnus. Weltz competed at Davis for two years before the school's swim program was cut. Although he never was at a swimming powerhouse and did not have much international experience before this year, he had a breakout performance at the U.S. Olympic Trials and then the Olympics.

Tabbed the "Accidental Olympian," Weltz trained with his collegiate coach and organized a highly specialized training regime that involved unique tactics, like using an ear chip as an aquatic metronome and reducing pool time to five days to allow for more rest. He used the skills he learned as an economics major at Davis to efficiently organize his training and specialize in his best stroke, breaststroke. By using what he learned in the classroom and in the pool, he surged to a shocking fifth-place finish at the Olympics.

Weltz is a great example of why education and athletics should go together. Perhaps a school might need to lower its academic standards to bring in these great athletes, but for everything that they bring to the table, I am absolutely convinced that it is the right thing to do.

While most of the athletes I know are recruited athletes, I am not one. I joined the varsity team as a walk-on because I love water polo and wanted to be on a team with some of the best players in the country. Playing water polo teaches me time management, teamwork and dedication that I will use for the rest of my life. Perhaps playing a sport might take away from time I spend writing papers or reading books, but it allows me to experience "Education through Athletics," the athletic department's motto, and learn things that aren't taught in the classroom.

Collegiate athletics throughout the country teach athletes valuable life skills, and most importantly, add a whole new dimension to student bodies. Recruiting high-level athletes makes "Education through Athletics" a reality.

Athletic Scholarships Benefit a School Financially

Douglas Brennan

Douglas Brennan is a student at Berkeley High School in California and a writer for the student newspaper, Berkeley High Jacket.

A recent trend in the college admissions process has seen colleges offering fewer merit based academic scholarships, but still a large number of athletic scholarships. Even though this trend may be seen as unfair to non-athletes applying to college, colleges should still continue to offer these athletic scholarships. There are many reasons why offering an increasing number of athletic scholarships at the expense of academic scholarships is both fair to applying students, and beneficial to the colleges.

A Diverse Student Body Benefits All

First of all, increasing the number of athletic scholarships allows many kids to attend college on the basis of their athletic excellence, who otherwise wouldn't be admitted solely on their academic pedigree. While many may see this as unfair, given that other "more academically qualified" students won't be able to attend the college, athletic scholarships lead to a student body that possesses a wider variety of skills and interests, resulting in a more well rounded, diverse school. When a college is more diverse, students have the opportunity to obtain a more complete education, because they get to experience and interact with many different types of people.

Second off, even though there may be a decreasing amount of money given out to students through academic scholarships, colleges are offering more and more financial aid to all of their students, thus enabling those who previously counted on academic scholarships to still be able to attend school. Furthermore, when putting together financial aid packages, colleges are including more grant aid and fewer student loans. Some schools, such as Princeton, now meet 100% of students' financial needs through grants. Across the board, the amount of grant aid being given out has significantly increased. From 2009 to 2010, students received 10 billion dollars more in Pell grant aid than they had the year before. In terms of overall financial aid, colleges are now helping students pay for college more so than they ever have before. Much of the increase in aid is due to the fact that many colleges are now "need blind" in their admission process, meaning that they don't factor in a student's ability to pay the tuition when making a decision about his or her application. Thus, after admitting a student, they are committing to meeting all of his or her demonstrated financial needs.

This is important because a student who is academically decorated enough to receive an academic scholarship will still be able to afford the college even if he or she isn't granted a merit-based academic scholarship. Therefore, despite the fact that there are fewer academic scholarships available to students, increases in financial aid, including grants, have helped to offset the consequences of the decreasing number of academic scholarships.

An Athletic Program Makes Money

Finally, from the perspective of the colleges, offering more athletic scholarships makes sense financially. This is because for a number of schools, strong athletic departments generate huge amounts of money (and increase school spirit) that can be used for many other expenditures and investment projects, like certain academic pursuits, to improve the school.

Naturally it is in the best interests of a university to offer more athletic scholarships in sports such as men's basketball and football in hopes of turning their teams into winners. It has been well documented that successful football and basketball programs can make big money for their colleges. For example, the University of Texas football program made over 93 million dollars for the school in 2011, and over 140 other football and basketball programs also made a huge amount of money. Given these statistics, it's easy for me to see why many colleges are offering more athletic scholarships in order to theoretically make money for the school. While many may argue that institutions of higher learning shouldn't be so focused on making money, colleges and universities are just like businesses in the sense that they must make money in order to continue operating and improving.

In conclusion, it is clear that offering more athletic scholarships at the expense of academic scholarships, when viewed in a larger context, is in fact fair to incoming students who are non-athletes, and beneficial to the colleges.

When Colleges Recruit Athletes, Everyone Loses

Jack Turnage

Jack Turnage is a student at the University of Texas at Austin.

Watching the London Olympic Games, I am particularly focused on the 17 Olympians from Princeton University. I am rooting wholeheartedly for them and all the other collegiate athletes on the U.S. squad. But as an incoming high school senior and an overoptimistically hopeful, athletically unexceptional Princeton applicant, I know that like athletes across the nation, Princeton's Olympians were probably given preferential access to their university. The recruitment of elite athletes from grade school onward is degrading our entire educational system, and it bodes ill not only for me and other academically oriented high schoolers but, more important, for America's children and our nation's future.

Most of us are taught that we need only perform well academically to get into college, but the uncomfortable reality is that America's institutions of higher education give athletes special access at the expense of gifted students. That is true even of top schools and those that are not allowed to offer scholarships. In *Reclaiming the Game: College Sports and Educational Values*, former Princeton President William Bowen and his co-authors describe how at 33 of America's most academically selective colleges, recruited athletes are nearly four times more likely to be admitted than other applicants of similar academic caliber. And such recruits are significantly more likely to be in the bottom third of their class.

Kids are not stupid. High schoolers and younger students and their parents see the commonplace success that athletes enjoy in college admissions, and kids understand that athletic prowess makes them far more likely to be admitted to a top school than does academic excellence alone. In fact, it is understood in high school that recruited athletes of even modest scholastic achievement regularly do better getting into select schools than their peers with much higher academic credentials.

What does this mean? It doesn't encourage students to excel academically. Rather, America's universities have brazenly created a perverse incentive for kids to focus on athletics from a very young age. After it becomes clear to a child that athletic skill maximizes his chance of being admitted to the college of his choice, that child will understandably focus on getting better at a sport. Not surprisingly, both students and parents are willing to sacrifice academic achievement and growth to get into a good college.

Far from leveling the playing field, college sports recruiting offers the moneyed a substantial advantage over less wealthy families.

Take one of my sister's friends, who last year as a 12-year-old made the cut for a highly selective club lacrosse team. Since then she has practiced intensively every day and traveled extensively for national tournaments. Her place on the team is continually reassessed, subjecting her to relentless pressure years before even beginning high school. She loves lacrosse, but she also knows that if she works hard enough she will have a college commitment by the end of the tenth grade—before taking a single standardized test and with less than two years of high school grades.

The giant American sports funnel results in upwards of 110,000 high schoolers per year receiving athletic scholarships to Division I and II schools, according to the NCAA. But how many millions of kids are steered toward sports early on in the hope of attaining admission to top colleges only to find that they aren't good enough, that their parents can't afford to pay for year-round travel and training, and that in the pursuit of athletic excellence they've neglected their academic goals and aspirations, perhaps irrevocably? How many wannabe recruits enter college acutely deficient in the skills critical to success there and later? And why, in the first place, should a rower or a football player be valued four times higher and singled out years earlier than an academically comparable piccolo player or aspiring physicist or debater?

Some will argue that athletics offers disadvantaged students a chance at a college education. But apart from a few sports like basketball and football, the vast majority of sports at the high school level are funded by parents through athletic clubs and require substantial financial resources. That is true for nearly all of the winter sports, like skiing and skating, as well as for ones like field hockey, swimming, and tennis. Far from leveling the playing field, college sports recruiting offers the moneyed a substantial advantage over less wealthy families.

After 40 months with unemployment above 8%, and with U.S. workers continuing to lose ground to global competitors, can America really afford to have its students rank 25th among industrialized nations in math and sciences? Instead of focusing on gold, shouldn't American universities be trying to outcompete China and India in producing science, technology, engineering, and math graduates?

This week I am cheering for all collegiate Olympians. But when London 2012 ends, I'll go back to hoping that Princeton admitted their competitors for their academic merit more than for their athletic prowess—for my own sake and for America's.

Preferential Admissions Treatment Is Harmful to Student Athletes

Thomas Emma

A former basketball captain at Duke University, Thomas Emma committed suicide in 2011.

For years controversy has swirled around the academic qualifications and performance of scholarship student/athletes. This has been especially true of athletes in the revenue-producing sports of football (at USC) [University of Southern California] and basketball (at Kentucky).

Everything from tax admission standards to low graduation rates to slide-through the classes and the tutors writing papers for players who have been publicized and scrutinized by the media ad nauseam.

In fact, rarely does a collegiate season go by in either football or basketball where some type of academic scandal doesn't make headlines. Coaches, athletic directors, and college administrators have weighed in on the subject as well. We find most of them pontificating on how student/athletes are improving their classroom marks and being vigilantly observed, making sure scholarship athletes go to class, attend study hall regularly, and behave like solid citizens.

What I almost never read or hear about is the athlete's perspective on student/athlete academics. Players, both current and former, are universally silent on the subject. I'm not quite sure why. But I am sure about the tremendous and unique academic challenges facing the elite, Division I scholarship athletes.

Many on the outside looking in erroneously believe that the college athletes at top programs should somehow be on par academically with the general student population.

This is false logic for a number of reasons. From my perspective as a former Division I college basketball player, I would like to touch on many of these reasons in detail.

Athletics Is Time-Consuming

Without a doubt, the biggest obstacle between scholarship basketball players and academic success is lack of time. With games, practices, travel, film/video sessions, weight training, injury/recovery treatments, media responsibilities, and alumni/community related duties, it's a wonder that athletes ever have time for anything outside of basketball during the competitive season.

And remember, most of these listed activities are much more time-consuming than they appear to be.

For instance, in addition to the hours on the court, basketball practice entails going to and from the gym, warming up, cooling down, showering, dressing, and engaging in some sanity-promoting locker-room banter.

Because of the popularity of college basketball and the huge number of media outlets in the country today . . . this represents quite a time commitment on the part of the players.

Travel includes packing, getting to and from the airport, dealing with delays, and, of course, missing and subsequently making up a fair share of class time.

Media obligations not only encompass the 15 to 20 minutes of post game Q & A, but numerous prearranged interviews set up by the schools sports information department as well.

Because of the popularity of college basketball and the huge number of media outlets in the country today (how many separate networks does ESPN have now, four, five?) this represents quite a time commitment on the part of the players.

And don't think for a second that these scheduled interviews are optional. While some old-school coaches like Bob Knight may choose to dwell on player availability in the name of academics, most programs welcome the free publicity and air time and use it as a recruiting tool.

I guess the best way for the lay person to understand how truly time-challenged basketball players are during the season is to give an example of a typical day:

Wake up is early, somewhere in the neighborhood of 7:00 a.m., give or take. Upon awakening, players must take physical inventory. This entails making sure that the inevitable in-season aches and pains did not manifest themselves into full-blown injuries overnight.

Provided everything is in working order, some light stretching follows. This 20-some odd minute ritual is necessary to get the body moving and the blood pumping in preparation for another physically demanding day.

Players are much less likely to injure themselves if their bodies begin the day loose and limber. Breakfast is next. Unlike the rank and file student, sleeping late and skipping breakfast even once in a while is not an option for the competitive basketball player.

Doing so would risk physical meltdown later in the day and contribute toward unwanted weight loss (most basketball players do all they can to maintain their body weight during the long, grueling season.)

Breakfast is followed by morning classes. Because of afternoon practice sessions, basketball players have to schedule most of their classes in the morning.

Once classes conclude, a hearty lunch follows. Again, all meals, including lunch, are required by players who hope to perform at their best later in the day at practice and still have some energy left after the basketball activities conclude.

From there, it's usually on to life maintenance chores such as laundry, shopping, room/apartment cleaning, etc. Keep in mind, that while the average student has his or her weekends basically free, college basketball players, because of games, practices, travel, etc. have no such luxury.

Before you know it, practice is looming and it's time to head over to the gym. Two to three hours of practice follow. As mentioned above, after the on-court action, the players often hit the weight room to pump iron, sit for film sessions/chalk talks, and engage in injury/recovery treatments.

After a hot shower, it's on to the training table to consume huge amounts of nutritious food to replenish an energy depleted body.

When the meal breaks, usually around 8:00 PM, it's time to hit the books, either at an organized study hall, the library, or in the privacy of a dorm room or apartment.

The pressure on big-time college athletes is immense in this day and age.

Needless to say, by the time the player sits down to study he is exhausted. Even staying awake is a worthy challenge.

Game days are no less busy. Between the game itself, players are required to appear at least 90 minutes before tip-off and the morning/midday shoot-around and the mandatory pre-game meal, so time for study can become severely limited.

Athletics Take a Physical and Emotional Toll

It should come as no surprise that participating in Division I college basketball is physically demanding. The cumulative physical toll throughout both fall and spring semesters is enormous and it eventually wreaks havoc on the player's ability to concentrate on his studies. . . .

While the physical toll of a long, grueling college basketball season is easily understandable, the emotional strain on young ballplayers is harder to quantify but just as prevalent. The pressure on big-time college athletes is immense in this day and age. Huge money and coaches jobs are often at stake and in the hands, to a large extent, of the players.

Division I college basketball players are regularly scrutinized by their coaches, their athletic directors, the student body, the alumni, the general fan population, and the local, regional, and national media.

And the pressures don't end there. Most players have huge hometown-fan followings as well.

This contingent, which includes family, high school friends, high school and AAU coaches, and so-called "advisors", are constantly in player's ears, imploring them to do this, do that, shoot more, pass less, etc.

The majority of the well meaning "advice", by the way, flies in the face of what team coaches want and expect. Some players, as I can attest from personal experience, even carry the expectations of entire towns on their backs.

All this can be extremely stressful and, by the way, a no-win situation for the athlete, as many townspeople actually expect the player to duplicate his high school success at the collegiate level. This, as we all know, rarely happens.

No less an authority than long-time college basketball broadcaster and analyst, Billy Packer, would seem to agree that stress can be brutal at the Division I level.

Packer, never one to mince words or be easy on players (or coaches for that matter), spoke frankly during last year's NCAA tournament on the subject.

He made a point to emphasize the tremendous emotional strain these young people were under, especially during tournament time. And remember, we're not talking about corporate executives or even seasoned professional athletes. We're talking about 18 to 22 year-old young men.

To make matters worse, every young player has his own unique stress threshold. Some are stress hardy and handle anything and everything in their path with equanimity; others are emotionally fragile, letting every little up and down affect their outlook (and performance); most are somewhere in the middle; all are hard to figure, since college-age youngsters are not the most communicative bunch.

The emotional turmoil that most Division I college basketball players endure over the course of a typical season makes staying on top of ones studies extremely difficult.

This, of course, makes it extremely difficult to recognize if an athlete is on the emotional edge. As such, coaches and other assisting personnel (assistant coaches, trainers, strength coaches, etc.) are often in the dark about a player's emotional state.

Conversely, physical fatigue is reasonably easy to detect. It shows up in the form of short jump shots, not getting back on defense, and missing free throws late in contests.

As you might expect, the emotional turmoil that most Division I college basketball players endure over the course of a typical season makes staying on top of ones studies extremely difficult.

Emotional equilibrium is a major factor in a human being's ability to concentrate on complicated subject matter (i.e., university level school work). The constant pressure from the outside, along with the ups (winning and performing well) and downs (losing and performing poorly) just doesn't allow for much in the way of emotional stability.

As such, basketball players can be expected at the very least to display uneven academic performance from early November through mid-March. Unfortunately this encompasses a good portion of the college school year.

Academic Competition Is Stiff

During my college athletic career, I had the opportunity to compete against some of the best amateur basketball players in the world, such as Charles Barkley, James Worthy, three-time national player of the year, Ralph Sampson, and a fellow named Michael Jordan.

The experience was rewarding, often frustrating (especially when guarding Jordan), and always exciting.

Who would have imagined, considering such names, that an equally difficult competition lay ahead for me elsewhere on campus?

Where you ask? In the classroom. What most college fans seem to forget is that at schools like Duke, Virginia, Stanford, and many others, the student body is comprised of the creme de la creme of academic achievers.

These young men and women are extremely talented and unequivocally prepared for the rigors of high level academia. They take their school work every bit as seriously as athletes take their games.

As such, basketball players, even those who come to college with above-average high school academic records, are not nearly up to par with these dedicated whiz kids.

To add some perspective, think of it this way: Take a top high school student who was accepted at Georgetown (or Duke, or Cal, or Georgia Tech, etc.) who also happened to be the sixth man on his reasonably successful high school team and match him up in a pick-up basketball game against a top freshmen basketball recruit.

Regardless of how hard he tries or how many hours he's spent practicing on the basketball court in between classes and study sessions, the rank and file student won't stand a chance against the prized recruit.

It's the same in the classroom. Expecting a middle of the road student to compete favorably with a high school valedictorian is, in a word, ridiculous.

Butting heads academically with these superior students is no different than trying to defend Michael Jordan on the fast break. It's intimidating and can lead to one falling behind in short order.

That's exactly what happened to me during my first semester freshman year at Duke. Before I had time to breathe I was behind the eight ball in most of my classes and struggling to stay afloat (i.e., stay academically eligible for the basketball season).

It certainly wasn't the professor's fault. Nor was I not trying my best. It was just that the large majority of my fellow classmates were so far ahead of me academically at the time that I couldn't keep up.

Throw into the mix that I was also adjusting to my first year of ACC basketball and it was not a pleasant initiation to college to say the least.

Only extra (hard) work with great tutors, an extremely helpful and understanding academic advisor, and a bit of old fashion good luck allowed me to continue my college experience past semester one.

So there you have it. The major reasons (as I see it) why scholarship college athletes have the odds stacked against them in the classroom. Hopefully, after reading this article you'll have a better understanding of what student athletes, basketball players more specifically, are up against academically at the university level.

As more eyes open to their challenges and struggles, more ideas and strategies will emerge to help them succeed not only in-between the lines of the playing field or court, but in the lecture halls, science labs, and classrooms as well.

CHAPTER 4

Should Standardized Tests Be a Factor in College Admissions?

Chapter Preface

Standardized testing for colleges began in 1900 with the formation of the College Entrance Examination Board by twelve prestigious universities who were concerned with the lack of a standard curriculum among New England boarding schools. The first test was administered in June 1901 to 973 students who would go on to apply to twenty-three colleges and universities. The College Board measured proficiency across nine subject areas and was considered a curriculum-based achievement test. A sample question from this test was the following:

> Write the rules for the following constructions and illustrate each by a Latin sentence:
>
> a.) Two uses of the dative
>
> b.) The cases used to indicate the relations of place
>
> c.) The cases used with verbs of remembering
>
> d.) The horatory (or jussive) subjunctive
>
> e.) The supine in urn.

A second educational milestone followed quickly with the invention of the first IQ test in 1905 by Alfred Binet, a French psychologist. During World War I, Harvard professor Robert Yerkes administered IQ tests to approximately 1.5 million recruits for the purpose of identifying officer candidates. Following the war, Carl Brigham, a psychologist at Princeton University, adapted the army intelligence test for higher education and marketed it to Ivy League schools and military academies. Brigham's test was called the Scholastic Aptitude Test and was given to more than eight thousand students on June 23, 1926. According to Richard C. Atkinson and Saul Geiser in "Reflections on a Century of College Admissions

Tests," Binet and Brigham "assumed that intelligence was a unitary, inherited attribute," and that "it was not subject to change over a lifetime and could be measured in a single number."[1] Unlike the curriculum-based College Boards, the Scholastic Aptitude Test measured aptitude, not subject mastery.

Harvard University president James Bryant Conant found Brigham's emphasis on aptitude over achievement to be compelling and Harvard began using the Scholastic Aptitude Test as a scholarship test in the 1930s. According to journalist and author Nicholas Lemann, during an interview on PBS's *Frontline* program:

> Conant had this kind of idealistic belief in creating a classless society. He was very, very tied to the idea of not favoring people who had been born into a privileged class, which is highly ironic today. So he thought that if you had tests that were achievement tests, or tests of mastery of the high school curriculum, it would be unfair to poor kids because they wouldn't have gone to good high schools. Anything that would help the rich kids who had been to fancy prep schools in the East Conant was against. So in his meetings with [assistant dean Henry] Chauncey about the SAT he would say over and over again, according to Chauncey, "Now are you sure this isn't an achievement test? Are you sure this is a pure aptitude test, pure intelligence? That's what I want to measure, because that is the way I think we can give poor boys the best chance to take away the advantage of rich boys."[2]

In 1944, the G.I. Bill for US veterans of World War II was made into law, making it financially possible for more than two million veterans to attend college during the next twelve years. By 1947, veterans accounted for 49 percent of all college

---

1. Richard C. Atkinson and Saul Geiser, "Reflections on a Century of College Admissions Tests," *Educational Researcher*, vol. 38, no. 9, December 2009.
2. Nicholas Lemann, "Secrets of the SAT," *Frontline*, October 4, 1999. http://www.pbs.org /wgbh/pages/frontline/shows/sats/interviews/lemann.html.

admissions. The Scholastic Aptitude Test gained widespread use as an efficient way of assessing the college-readiness of this exponentially larger pool of applicants. The test was also consistent with American ideals of meritocracy, as it was perceived to provide an objective way of measuring the potential of students from high schools of wide-ranging quality.

Over the years, the Scholastic Aptitude Test has been modified to reflect changes in educational philosophy. In 1930 the test was split into two parts—a verbal aptitude and a math aptitude section, a format that would continue until 2004. In 1990 the Scholastic Aptitude Test was renamed the Scholastic Assessment Test and in 1996 was called only by its acronym SAT, a renaming that the College Board said was designed to "correct the impression among some people that the SAT measures something that is innate and impervious to change regardless of effort or instruction"—a direct contradiction to the early goals of the test.

During the 1990s, an examination of college admissions policies at the University of California system revealed some surprising data about the SAT. According to Atkinson and Geiser:

> Far from promoting equity and access in college admissions, we found that—compared with traditional indications of academic achievement—the SAT had a more adverse impact on low-income and minority applicants. The SAT was more closely correlated than other indicators with socioeconomic status and so tended to diminish the chances of admission for underrepresented minority applicants.[3]

Research also found that the SAT was a relatively poor predictor of college success compared to high school grades as well as curriculum-based achievement tests.

A specific example of a question biased against low-income applicants was the analogy question correctly identifying oars-

---

3. op cit.

man and regatta as having a similar relationship to runner and marathon. In the mid-1990s, analogy questions were replaced by short reading passages and open-ended math questions were introduced.

The most recent significant change to the SAT came in 2005. Prompted by issues raised by the University of California study, a revised test called the SAT-R, with R standing for "reasoning," was launched. The major change is the incorporation of a writing exam.

Despite the evolution of the SAT over the years to reflect changes in society and educational theory, the high-stakes test remains controversial. In the following chapter, commentators, educators, and journalists debate the value of the SAT in predicting college success, and whether or not the test is biased against minorities, women, and the socioeconomically disadvantaged.

My View:
10 Reasons the SAT Matters

Kathryn Juric

Kathryn Juric is vice president of the College Board's SAT program.

The College Board created the SAT to democratize access to higher education by providing an objective measure for evaluating a student's college readiness. This function has endured for more than 80 years and for those who doubt its value, here are 10 reasons why the SAT continues to be an integral part of the college admission process:

Why the SAT Matters

1. The SAT has a proven track record as a fair and valid predictor of first-year college success for all students, regardless of gender, race, or socio-economic status. The most recent validity study [2007] utilizing data from more than 150,000 students at more than 100 colleges and universities demonstrates that the combined use of SAT and high school GPA is a better predictor of college success than HSGPA alone.

2. The SAT gives students the opportunity to demonstrate their college-preparedness despite inconsistent grading systems throughout the nation's high schools. And SAT scores provide a national, standardized benchmark that neutralizes the risk of grade inflation.

3. The SAT tests students' ability to apply what they have learned in high school and to problem-solve based on that knowledge—skills that are critical to success in college and the workforce. The College Board conducts regular curriculum surveys to ensure the content tested on the SAT reflects the content being taught in the nation's high school classrooms.

4. Despite what some testing critics have said, colleges still depend on college entrance exams as part of the admission process. According to a 2010 survey published by the National Association of College Admission Counseling, admissions officers ranked college entrance exam scores as the third-most important factor in the admission process—behind only grades in college prep courses and the strength of the student's high school curriculum.

5. The SAT actually shines a spotlight on the inequities in education by putting every student on equal footing. The notion that the differences in test scores among different groups of students is somehow the result of testing bias is an idea that is "universally rejected within mainstream psychology," according to University of Minnesota researchers.

6. Unlike other standardized tests intended to measure a student's college-readiness, the SAT requires a writing portion of the exam, an essential skill in today's e-communications era.

7. While organizations that oppose standardized testing might suggest otherwise, nearly all four-year colleges require a college entrance exam, and some "test-optional" schools do, in fact, consider SAT scores in the admission process when students submit them. Data provided by colleges and universities to college-planning

sites such as BigFuture.org show that many test-optional schools receive SAT scores from a majority of the students who ultimately matriculate at those institutions. For instance, of the students who were admitted to and enrolled at Bowdoin last year, more than 70% submitted SAT scores as part of the admission process.

8. Parents and students should keep in mind that colleges do not base admission decisions on test scores alone. The College Board has always advocated that the best use of the SAT is in combination with high school grades and other valid measures, as part of a holistic and comprehensive review of a student's overall fit for a particular institution.

9. States and districts can use aggregate SAT scores in conjunction with other measures to evaluate the general direction of education in a particular district or state, develop curriculum, and determine staffing needs. The SAT is the only college readiness measure statistically linked to NAEP, the Nation's Report Card.

10. As part of its commitment to access and equity in education, the College Board introduced the SAT Fee-Waiver Program more than 40 years ago to assist those students for whom test fees presented an obstacle in the college-going process. Today, more than 20% of SAT takers utilize fee waivers, including more than 350,000 students in the graduating class of 2011 alone. During the 2010–2011 academic year, the College Board provided more than $37 million in free SAT services.

In Defense of the SAT

Po Bronson

Po Bronson is a columnist for Newsweek.com and the author of a number of books, including The First $20 Million Is Always the Hardest.

One of the most popular ideas of our time is the notion that in judging a young person's future success, we've become imbalanced, giving too much credence to whether a child has learned the stuff of textbooks, and too little value to whether that child has learned the stuff of real life.

The latter is a whole constellation of behaviors and skills, from creativity to emotional-intelligence to self-discipline to practical judgment. In this modern paradigm, the elements of real life success are characterized as highly generalizable, useful everywhere from the urban street corner to the boardroom. Meanwhile, the elements that go into book learning are characterized as being narrowly applicable, useful only for getting into college, at which point the other factors take over.

No matter who is making this argument—whether it's Daniel Goleman, Dan Pink, Robert Sternberg, Malcolm Gladwell, Thomas Stanley, or some college president—it always stands on a few key bricks. One of those bricks is that the SAT doesn't predict much of anything.

It's commonly said that the SAT, taken in a senior year of high school, has only about a 40% correlation with a student's freshman year college GPA. If it's that bad at predicting how well a kid does in college, just one year later, then how could it predict longer-term outcomes in life, when other factors become increasingly important? The SAT is designed, specifically, to screen for college success—if it doesn't accomplish what it's built for, then surely something else (that's not being tested) accounts for real success, in college and in life.

Using this argument, the door is opened for all these other variables to be postulated as the new basis for success.

I've always had a skeptical feeling about the 40% correlation statistic, and so I've never relied on it or used it in print. There are two self-selection problems that make it really hard to control the data. First, high schoolers of diverging abilities apply to different schools—the strongest students apply to one tier of colleges, and the average students apply to a less ambitious tier, with some overlap. Second, once students get to a college, they enroll in classes they believe they can do well in. Many of the strongest students try their hand at Organic Chemistry, while more of the less-confident students take Marketing 101. At each of these colleges and courses, students might average a B grade, but the degree of difficulty in achieving that B is not comparable.

It turns out that an SAT score is a far better predictor than everyone has said.

Many scholars have attempted to control for these issues, looking at data from a single college or a single required course that all freshman have to take, and their work has suggested the 40% correlation is a significant underestimate. I've long wondered what would happen if an economist really took on this massive mathematical mess, on a large scale, harvesting data from a wide selection of universities.

Finally this has been done, by Christopher Berry of Wayne State University and Paul Sackett of the University of Minnesota. They pulled 5.1 million grades, from 167,000 students, spread out over 41 colleges. They also got the students' SAT scores from the College Board, as well as the list of schools each student asked the College Board to send their SAT scores to, an indicator of which colleges they applied to. By isolating the overlaps—where students had applied to the same colleges, and taken the same courses at the same time with the same instructor—they extracted a genuine apples-to-apples subset of data.

It turns out that an SAT score is a far better predictor than everyone has said. When properly accounting for the self-selection bias, SAT scores correlate with college GPA around 67%. In the social sciences, that's considered a great predictor.

My point isn't that other life variables don't matter. Some of the success factors that have been touted are certainly additive to what's tested by the SAT. It's still worthwhile to explore why people succeed, both at school and in real life. But we may not be imbalanced; our valuing of differing abilities may be right on target. Meanwhile, the argument all these alternative success-factors are built on needs repair.

The SAT Is Not Racially Biased

Cherylyn Harley LeBon

Cherylyn Harley LeBon is president and chief executive officer of KLAR Strategies, a public affairs firm. She is also the co-chairwoman of the Project 21 National Advisory Board of the National Leadership Network of Black Conservatives.

It's September, so it's back-to-school for American kids and other children around the world. Many families pack away the swimsuits and beach gear, unpack the notebooks, lunch bags, brand new shoes, and look forward to the regular routine.

The SAT Is Not Racially Biased

This fall is also an interesting time of reflection in our country.

Record numbers of Americans are living below the poverty line, the housing foreclosure rate continues to climb, and rising unemployment will, in fact, keep some of these children going back to school on the school lunch program longer than expected. In these desperate times, people resort to desperate measures—engaging in scare tactics and myths so often embraced and perpetuated by the liberal media. Chief among these myths is the controversy surrounding the SAT college admissions test. Disturbingly, the media's promotion of this myth is creating confusion among students and families considering college options.

Opponents of the SAT test argue that the test determines who gets into college and who does not, and should be, therefore, abolished in favor of "test optional policies." This argument is largely promoted by the group Fair Test, which advocates an end to standardized testing in college admissions.

Fair Test's roster of supporters includes George Soros, the infamous billionaire who has bankrolled MoveOn.org and several other left-wing groups and politicians. Fair Test touts itself as an educational organization, but it is a special interest group recognized by the mainstream media as a credible source on educational testing issues.

The sad result of this misinformation is the effect on students and families preparing for college, particularly students and families of color. Fair Test continues to argue that the SAT is biased against minority and low income students. In fact, the goal of Fair Test is to play the blame game and portray minority students (or any students who do not perform well on the SAT) as victims in their sandbox game of Limousine Liberal politics.

The racial bias myth was definitively laid to rest several years ago in the peer-reviewed journal *American Psychologist*. University of Minnesota researchers Paul Sackett, Matthew Borneman and Brian Connelly examined the issue and reported that any inference that group scores are linked to bias is, "unequivocally rejected within mainstream psychology." The only people still advocating that the SAT is racially biased are patriarchal liberal groups including Fair Test who play the race card when other options fail.

The truth is, every SAT question is exhaustively pretested and carefully analyzed for any bias.

Others have also refuted the claims of racial bias in standardized testing.

In 2008, Jonathan Epstein, a researcher with Maguire Associates, studied the impact of test-optional policies in college admissions. Epstein discovered that test-optional policies at colleges and universities lead to artificially inflated average SAT scores among incoming freshmen. He found this resulted in further confusion for prospective students and families and "is not in the best interest of any institution or higher education in general."

Racial Score Differences Are Due to Unequal K-12 Education

As parents, we all want our children to grow up and become productive members of society. The college search process is an important step in helping our children make major life decisions. A political group is advocating for the end of standardized testing, and continues to mislead students and families by attempting to influence an academic professional organization overseeing college admissions. The result will be to marginalize successful black students or those who come from other racial, ethnic or socioeconomic groups.

Promoting the racial bias myth also harms students by creating the wrong expectation that the deck is stacked against them. The truth is, every SAT question is exhaustively pretested and carefully analyzed for any bias.

Questions are reviewed by panels of K-12 and college educators and questions which indicate any bias are never used in the actual test. Furthermore, more than three-quarters of the nation's top historically black colleges and universities accept the SAT as an admissions requirement. Score differences may exist among some students in different groups, but they do not indicate bias in the SAT, and are an unfortunate reflection of inequities in K-12 education across thousands of school districts.

The continued claims of racial bias in SAT testing are insulting to all families of color when interest groups portray us as victims incapable of advocating for ourselves. The policies of Fair Test and other liberal interest groups reveal that these

groups are more concerned with the politics of race than edu-
cating the children of this country.

Standardized Tests Tend to Favor Upper-Class Students

Cooper Aspegren

Cooper Aspegren is news editor of The Oracle.

Performance on the SAT is one of the most significant factors in a college's decision to admit or deny a student from enrollment. Because organizations like *U.S. News and World Report* rank universities based on the distribution of freshmen SAT scores, colleges seek to admit students who perform highly on the SAT as a means of increasing their prestige. This approach, however, excludes too many students with lower socioeconomic status (SES) from standing a chance at earning an acceptance letter. The format and competition involved in SAT test taking significantly and undeservedly inhibits the ability of socioeconomically disadvantaged students to successfully enroll in the college of their choice.

Upper-Class Students Get an Unfair Advantage

A student's SES has long been linked to his or her performance on the SAT. Cumulative findings even pushed the College Board, the company that finances and operates the SAT, to eliminate the analogy portion which involved comparisons of two different sets of words, from the critical reading section in 2003. Critics beforehand had complained that only wealthy students could correctly answer a question involving crew, a sport typically pursued by higher-class members of society. The particular question required test takers to equate an "oarsman" with a "runner" and a "regatta" with a "marathon." Even after the removal of the analogy section, research from the Harvard University Educational Review and other academic media still found 200 to 300 point discrepancies in the performances of advantaged and disadvantaged students, on the critical reading and writing sections in particular. These studies serve as clear links to the test's inherent socioeconomic bias.

Without eliminating its inherent bias, the SAT will continue to lose what is left of its relevance.

Socioeconomically disadvantaged test-takers simply cannot afford the benefits of SAT preparation services in the form of private tutors or classes that cost thousands of dollars. Without outside help to prepare for the test, socioeconomically disadvantaged students cannot enjoy the same increase in score as can their more privileged contemporaries. Many socioeconomically disadvantaged students therefore cannot reach the interquartile SAT score range of the school of their choice; as a result, they are unfairly forced to dial down on their college aspirations. Researchers have also noticed that a higher income leads students to a far greater breadth and depth of personal and academic experience independent of test tutoring, ultimately equating with a higher SAT score. Without this level of experience and opportunity, socioeconomically underprivileged students face an unjust disadvantage.

The College Board's defense of its administration of the SAT lies in evidence that the test accurately indicates a student's performance at the college level. However, Princeton University researchers have found that other academic factors, such as class rank, serve as more precise predictors.

The fact that the SAT bars so many students with potential on the basis of socioeconomic status makes its ultimate importance and usefulness far from certain. Recently, universities have started to take notice. Ahead of the fall 2012 admissions process, Sarah Lawrence College chose to make the SAT an optional component of a freshman application rather than one that was automatically not considered. Another option some colleges have turned to is to consider denoting SAT score submission as non-required. Schools like Bowdoin College, American University, College of the Holy Cross and Pitzer College have already taken this route, while the UC system and even Harvard University are considering to do so in the future. Without eliminating its inherent bias, the SAT will continue to lose what is left of its relevance.

New Evidence of Racial Bias on SAT

Scott Jaschik

Scott Jaschik is the founder and editor of Inside Higher Ed.

A new study may revive arguments that the average test scores of black students trail those of white students not just because of economic disadvantages, but because some parts of the test result in differential scores by race for students of equal academic prowess.

The finding—already being questioned by the College Board—could be extremely significant as many colleges that continue to rely on the SAT may be less comfortable doing so amid allegations that it is biased against black test-takers.

"The confirmation of unfair test results throws into question the validity of the test and, consequently, all decisions based on its results. All admissions decisions based exclusively or predominantly on SAT performance—and therefore access to higher education institutions and subsequent job placement and professional success—appear to be biased against the African American minority group and could be exposed to legal challenge," says the study, which has just appeared in *Harvard Educational Review*.

The existence of racial patterns on SAT scores is hardly new. The average score on the reading part of the SAT was 429 for black students last year—99 points behind the average for white students. And while white students' scores were flat, the average score for black students fell by one. Statistics like these are debated every year when SAT data are released, and when similar breakdowns are offered on other standardized tests.

The standard explanation offered by defenders of the tests is that the large gaps reflect the inequities in American society—since black students are less likely than white students to attend well-financed, generously-staffed elementary and secondary schools, their scores lag.

In other words, the College Board says that American society is unfair, but the SAT is fair. And while many educators question that fairness of using a test on which wealthier students do consistently better than less wealthy students, research findings that directly isolate race as a factor in the fairness of individual SAT questions have, of late, been few.

The new paper in fact is based on a study that set out to replicate one of the last major studies to do so—a paper published in the *Harvard Educational Review* in 2003, strongly attacked by the College Board—and the new paper confirms those results (but using more recent SAT exams). The new paper is by Maria Santelices, assistant professor of education at the Catholic University of Chile, and Mark Wilson, professor of education at the University of California at Berkeley. The earlier study was by Roy Freedle of the Educational Testing Service.

The [2000 and 2010] studies suggest scores for black students [on the SAT] are being held down by the way the test is scored.

The focus of both studies is on questions that show "differential item functioning," known by its acronym DIF. A DIF question is one on which students "matched by proficiency" and other factors have variable scores, predictably by race, on selected questions. A DIF question has notable differences between black and white (or, in theory, other subsets of students) whose educational background and skill set suggest that they should get similar scores. The 2003 study and this year's found no DIF issues in the mathematics section.

But what Freedle found in 2003 has now been confirmed independently by the new study: that some kinds of verbal questions have a DIF for black and white students. On some of the easier verbal questions, the two studies found that a DIF favored white students. On some of the most difficult verbal questions, the DIF favored black students. Freedle's theory about why this would be the case was that easier questions are likely reflected in the cultural expressions that are used commonly in the dominant (white) society, so white students have an edge based not on education or study skills or aptitude, but because they are most likely growing up around white people. The more difficult words are more likely to be learned, not just absorbed.

While the studies found gains for both black and white students on parts of the SAT, the white advantage is larger such that the studies suggest scores for black students are being held down by the way the test is scored and that a shift to favor the more difficult questions would benefit black test-takers.

The new study is based on data for students who enrolled at the University of California system across several administrations of the SAT—with versions used subsequent to Freedle's article. (The new research is the result of a study the authors undertook at the request of University of California officials, and they note in the paper that despite the request for information from the University of California, it took two years for the College Board to provide the data needed.) While the new study found the same DIF that Freedle did, an attempt to find a DIF for Latino students failed to show one.

But, the authors write, that doesn't minimize the significance of their findings that back the study from 2003 that the College Board has said wasn't accurate. "Although our findings limit the phenomenon observed to the verbal test and the African American subgroup, these findings are important because they show that the SAT, a high-stakes test with significant consequences for the educational opportunities available to young people in the United States, favors one ethnic group over another," write Santelices and Wilson.

"Neither the specifics of the method used to study differential item functioning nor the date of the test analyzed invalidate Freedle's claims that the SAT treats African American minorities unfairly."

Kathleen Fineout Steinberg, a spokeswoman for the College Board, said that just as the organization disagreed with the 2003 study, so it does with the new research. She questioned whether the California sample could be seen as broad enough to draw conclusions on, and said that some of the tests examined had less of a DIF than others, raising questions about the assumptions made. She called the *Harvard Educational Review* study an example of "presenting inconsistent findings as conclusive fact."

She said every test question used on the SAT is subjected to rigorous analysis (before use) to weed out any that would not be fair to all test takers. "We believe that our test is fair," she said. "It is rigorously researched, probably the most rigorously researched standardized test in the world."

As to the persistence of score differences, Steinberg said that this is not because of the test. "There certainly are subgroup differences in scores," she said. "We recognize that and acknowledge it. It's a reflection of educational inequity. It's something we are concerned with." She also said that the College Board welcomes research on the SAT, but viewed the Freedle study as having been "discredited," and said that nothing in the new study changed that view.

The College Board's tough stance on Freedle's research is not new—and was recounted by Jay Matthews in an article in 2003 in *The Atlantic Monthly....*

Robert Schaeffer, public education director of the National Center for Fair and Open Testing, a long-time critic of the SAT, called the new research "a bombshell," and said that the study "presents a profound challenge to institutions which still rely heavily on the SAT to determine undergraduate admissions or scholarship awards."

Schaeffer said that he agreed with the authors of the new study that use of the SAT could face legal challenges, given that this study now backs the finding that some of its questions may be harmful to the scores of black test-takers. While the College Board says colleges aren't supposed to rely too much on the SAT, and most colleges that require the SAT say that they use it only as one factor among many, Schaeffer and others have doubted those claims.

"A shrewd litigator could use this study and the process of discovery to find out a lot more about how colleges use the test and, at a minimum, embarrass them," he said.

More broadly, he said that with more colleges considering ending SAT requirements, this new study is "another strong argument" for doing so. "It's going to add to the momentum."

Marist College will be announcing this week that it is ending its SAT requirement, joining many others that have done so.

Standardized Tests Discriminate Against Minority and Lower Income Students

Joseph Soares, interviewed by Sarah Ovaska

Joseph Soares is a sociology professor at Wake Forest University. Sarah Ovaska is an investigative reporter at NC Policy Watch, a nonprofit and nonpartisan research and news organization located in North Carolina.

Joseph Soares, a sociology professor at Wake Forest University, has been a vocal critic of the use of standardized tests in the college admission process.

Test Scores Favor Wealthier Students

Soares' research has found that tests like the ACTs and SATs put low-income and minority students at significant disadvantages and have resulted in a lack of diversity at the nation's four-year colleges, including public universities in the UNC [University of North Carolina] system. He thinks high school grade point averages would give admissions counselors a better grasp of a student's abilities without the gender and racial biases that test scores carry.

Soares shared his thoughts recently with N.C. Policy Watch, and told us why he thinks North Carolina's public university system should turn its back on the ACTs and SATs.

[NC Policy Watch]: *Is the University of North Carolina at Chapel Hill, the state's flagship university, serving poor and rich students equally?*

[Joseph Soares]: No. UNC-Chapel Hill's student population has the same economic composition of an elite private college. At UNC-Chapel Hill, 72 percent of undergraduates come from families with incomes in the top quartile of North Carolinians; the national average for private colleges is 79 percent.

Also at Chapel Hill, only 12 percent of the students come from families in the bottom half of North Carolina's incomes.

We are missing out on a lot of talent that would benefit our state's human capital and economic welfare and we need to get more youths from the bottom half of our families into our public universities.

Why do students from higher-income families have a better chance of getting into UNC-Chapel Hill than those from poorer families?

Admissions that rely on test scores more than high school grades generate a student body that is biased toward students from higher incomes and against those from lower incomes and racial minorities.

Independent researchers, and even the testing agencies themselves, all agree that high school grades have always worked better than test scores in predicting college grades. It is a myth that grade inflation or quality variations between high schools reduces or eliminates the statistical superiority of high school grades over standardized tests.

High school grades reflect years of effort and are a more reliable assessment of college potential than test scores.

[The SAT] is a more reliable predictor of demographics than it is of academic performance.

In my book "SAT Wars: The Case for Test-Optional College Admissions," there is a chapter written by the emeritus president of the University of California, Richard Atkinson, and his statistical colleague, Saul Geiser, where they point out this fact.

Geiser and Atkinson wrote, "Irrespective of the quality or type of school attended, cumulative grade point average (GPA) in academic subjects in high school has proved to be the best overall predictor of student performance in college. This finding has been confirmed in the great majority of "predictive-validity" studies conducted over the years, including studies conducted by the testing agencies themselves."

Which students are disadvantaged by tests like ACTs or SATs?

Everyone who is not from a family in the top 10 percent of the income distribution. In addition, all blacks, Hispanics and women are disadvantaged by this test. The test is a more reliable predictor of demographics than it is of academic performance.

High school grades are not as compromised by social demographics as test scores. For example, test scores correlate with family income, which means the higher one's family income, the higher one's test score. Meanwhile, high school GPAs have no correlation to family income. SAT and ACT scores show large and growing demographic disparities by race, gender, and family incomes.

High School Grades Are a Better Measure

Why use a statistically weak measure, test scores, when they transmit so much social bias when the most statistically reliable measure, high schools grades, do not?

The unfair impact of test scores, putting most American families at a disadvantage, was the reason the National Association for College Admissions Counselors urged all colleges to consider going test optional in 2008 national report that found, "test scores appear to calcify differences based on class, race/ethnicity, and parental educational attainment."

If high school GPAs work better, then why are so many colleges still using standardized tests?

Ignorance, complacency, and competitive pressures. In this age of academic specialization, most professors and administrators do not know that high school GPAs works better. When deans are aware, that information doesn't always translate into action. I have been told by admissions deans that they are aware that test scores are not better predictors of college grades than high school GPAs, yet they claim their faculty resists change because of the mistaken belief that the test is a measure of IQ. Faculty also do not want to "lower standards" by dropping a test that the vast majority of faculty did well on.

Test-optional institutions (schools that don't require SAT or ACT scores for admission) are not a deviant "hippy" minority. When Wake Forest University went test-optional in 2009, there were about 750 test-optional colleges. Today there are over 870, representing nearly 40 percent of all four-year degree-granting colleges in America. We are a growing movement in higher education and a tipping point will be reached in the foreseeable future when everyone will rush to join us.

What is working in other states to allow students from disadvantaged backgrounds access to higher education?

Texas' 10 percent scholarship program, where all youth in the top 10 percent of each high school are automatically eligible and receive partial scholarships to attend University of Texas at Austin. That program works well to capture social diversity.

California has adopted a similar policy and has a good "master plan" in which the top 9 percent of high school graduates are given spots in the University of California system; the next 12 percent can go in to the California State system; and everyone else is eligible for California's excellent community colleges.

What advice or comments do you have for UNC system leaders who are currently working on a strategic plan with specific degree attainment goals?

There is a great need for public universities to reconnect with high schools in the state, setting standards and having a place for each high school graduate in the public higher educational system.

If we had public university admissions based on high school records, we would keep our youth focused on learning real academic materials and we'd save our taxpayers and their children money, test prep stress, and anxiety. It would be a win-win situation for public education. We would end up with better high schools and a fairer, more transparent public university admissions system.

GPA, SAT, ACT ... RIP

Brandon Busteed

Brandon Busteed is the executive director of Gallup Education.

It's time to end our obsession with standardized testing and grade point averages. We've spent the better part of the last two decades—with an almost myopic focus—trying to improve these measures across our educational system. Despite national efforts to raise test scores through initiatives such as No Child Left Behind, there has been little-to-no improvement in scores. We have also witnessed rampant grade inflation, with average college GPAs, for example, rising from 2.3 to 3.2 in the past few decades, making their value suspect.

In the meantime, a mountain of evidence and sentiment is building that these measures may not be very strong predictors of success, and that other measures—like student engagement and hope—may be much better.

Take, for example, the powerful results from a new survey of 2,586 superintendents: the leaders of our K-12 school districts just essentially voted "no confidence" on GPA and standardized tests as strong predictors of college success. In fact, only 6% of superintendents strongly agree that SAT and ACT scores are the best predictors of college success, and only 5% of them strongly agree GPA is the best predictor. Americans also say No Child Left Behind has hurt more than helped.

Paul Tough's book *How Children Succeed* has shed light on other measures of success, like "grit" and "resilience." Sir Ken Robinson has become a global force on education redesign by arguing that we have lost track of things like encouraging creativity in schools. And Google announced last week that they are no longer taking into account job candidates' test scores and grades, because they found no relationship between those measures and performance on the job. This buzz around a new focus to affect student success is supported by some of Gallup's best research, for example, that the three constructs of hope, engagement, and wellbeing account for as much as one-third of the variance in student success. Yet our nation's schools are not paying attention to these kinds of things. What we're starting to learn is that "soft skills" and "social-emotional" learning are pretty important. There's a case that the "soft stuff" may be the best measures of all.

America's economy is fundamentally about entrepreneur-ship—boldly and bravely striking out in new directions. But we have lost sight of that in our schools and colleges.

The biggest problem with standardized testing is that it seeks standardized answers. We're not just overinvesting in standardized testing, we're actually testing standardization. That is to say, most standardized tests are designed to have students come up with the same answers. We're teaching them how to be similar, not different. And although we need to test certain competencies and intelligence, it is becoming quite clear that there are many kinds of competencies and many forms of intelligence that we are not picking up on with our current testing approaches.

Gallup's work on strengths development has shown that every human on the planet has a unique talent signature—like a fingerprint. And we've found that each person's success is best determined by how well they leverage their unique talents on a daily basis. Not by trying to be the same as others. And not by trying to "fix their weaknesses."

As a parent, I want my kids to be uncommon, not common. I want them to be unique, not the same. I want them to discover different solutions to the problem, as opposed to the same answer. As an education expert, I want my country to espouse the same. America's economy is fundamentally about entrepreneurship—boldly and bravely striking out in new directions. But we have lost sight of that in our schools and colleges. We have a system that encourages the opposite—working within narrowly defined rules, teaching to the test, and we are ultimately aiming at standardized answers and outcomes.

To be clear, this is not to suggest that we wholesale abandon standardized testing. These tests should be part of a much more balanced scorecard that includes many other more important measures. But we do need to greatly deemphasize the role these assessments currently play.

As scary as it may sound, we need to stop worrying about how America stacks up on PISA scores compared with other countries. Parents need to stop obsessing over their kids' performance on tests and the grades they get. Teachers need to stop teaching to the test. And our educational leaders need to push into new frontiers where they can measure (and espouse) more of what matters the most.

Based on decades of Gallup's best science and research, we have a simple proposal for how we can get back on the path to winning again in education. And what the new Bill of Rights for all students should be. The path is much more about getting back to the basics than about doing something radically new. We need to care more about each student as a unique person. We need to help them discover what they like to do. We need to help them discover what they're best at. None of that is helped by standardized testing. Time to put to rest our favorite acronyms of accountability in education. RIP SAT, ACT, and GPA!

Organizations to Contact

The editors have compiled the following list of organizations concerned with the issues debated in this book. The descriptions are derived from materials provided by the organizations. All have publications or information available for interested readers. The list was compiled on the date of publication of the present volume; the information provided here may change. Be aware that many organizations take several weeks or longer to respond to inquiries, so allow as much time as possible.

Brookings Institution
1775 Massachusetts Ave. NW, Washington, DC   20036-2188
(202) 797-6000 • fax: (202) 797-6004
e-mail: communications@brookings.edu
website: www.brookings.edu

Founded in 1927, the Brookings Institution conducts research and publishes in the fields of government, foreign policy, economics, social sciences, and education. The organization publishes the *Brookings Review* quarterly as well as numerous books and research papers, including the Brookings Policy Brief Series. It also has published a number of articles on affirmative action in education.

Center for Equal Opportunity (CEO)
7700 Leesburg Pike, Suite 231, Falls Church, VA   22043
(703) 442-0066 • fax: (703) 442-0449
website: www.ceousa.org

The Center for Equal Opportunity (CEO) is a conservative think tank concerned with issues of race and ethnicity. It is opposed to admissions and hiring practices that are based on race and ethnicity, and it also opposes bilingual education. CEO publishes a number of papers opposing the practice of affirmative action in education and business, many of which are available at its website.

College Board
45 Columbus Ave., New York, NY   10023
(212) 713-8000
website: www.collegeboard.org

The College Board is a not-for-profit membership association whose mission is to connect students to college success and opportunity. It is composed of more than 5,900 schools, colleges, universities, and other educational organizations. It sells such standardized tests as the SAT, SAT Subject, PSAT, and Advanced Placement. Its publications include *The Official SAT Study Guide, College Handbook,* and *Book of Majors.*

Educational Testing Service (ETS)
660 Rosedale Rd., Princeton, NJ   08541
(609) 921-9000 • fax: (609) 734-5410
website: www.ets.org

The Educational Testing Service (ETS) is a testing and assessment organization that develops, administers, and scores more than fifty million standardized tests annually in more than 180 countries. Among these standardized tests are the SAT, Graduate Record Exam (GRE), and Test of English as a Foreign Language (TOEFL).

National Association for College Admission Counseling (NACAC)
1050 North Highland St., Suite 400, Arlington, VA   22201
(703) 836-2222 • fax: (703) 243-9375
e-mail: info@nacacnet.org
website: www.nacacnet.org

Founded in 1937, the National Association for College Admission Counseling (NACAC) is an association of more than thirteen thousand counseling and college admissions professionals. The organization publishes articles on the benefits of a diverse student body and is supportive of the consideration of race and ethnicity in the college admissions process. Among its publications is the quarterly *Journal of College Admission.*

National Center for Fair and Open Testing
PO Box 300204, Jamaica Plain, MA 02130
(617) 477-9792
website: www.fairtest.org

The National Center for Fair and Open Testing, also known as FairTest, is an organization that advocates for the reform of current standardized testing and assessment practices in education and employment. It publishes a regular electronic newsletter, the *Examiner*, plus a full catalog of materials on both K-12 and university testing to aid teachers, administrators, students, parents, and researchers.

National Center for Public Policy and Higher Education
152 North Third St., Suite 705, San Jose, CA 95112
(408) 271-2699 • fax: (408) 271-2697
e-mail: center@highereducation.org
website: www.highereducation.org

The National Center for Public Policy and Higher Education promotes public policies that enhance Americans' opportunities to pursue education and training beyond high school. The Center prepares action-oriented analyses of policy issues facing the states and the nation regarding opportunity and achievement in higher education. It also communicates performance results and key findings to the public and civic, business, and higher education leaders, along with state and federal officials.

National Education Association (NEA)
1201 16th St. NW, Washington, DC 20036-3290
(202) 833-4000 • fax: (202) 822-7974
website: www.nea.org

The National Education Association (NEA) is a volunteer-based organization that represents 3.2 million public school teachers, university and college faculty members, college students training to be teachers, retired educators, and other educational professionals. Its mission is to advocate for educational professionals and to support the goal of public education to prepare every student to succeed in a diverse world. It publishes books, newsletters, e-newsletters, and magazines, including its flagship publication, *NEAToday Magazine.*

Public Agenda

6 East 39th St., 9th Floor, New York, NY   10016
(212) 686-6610 • fax: (212) 889-3461
e-mail: info@publicagenda.org
website: www.publicagenda.org

Public Agenda is a nonpartisan organization that researches public opinion and produces informational materials on policy issues. Its reports on standardized testing include *Reality Check 2006: Is Support for Standards and Testing Fading?* and *Survey Finds Little Sign of Backlash Against Academic Standards or Standardized Tests.*

US Department of Education

400 Maryland Ave. SW, Washington, DC   20202
(800) 872-5327
website: www.ed.gov

The US Department of Education was created in 1980 by combining offices from several federal agencies. The department's mission is to promote student achievement and preparation for global competitiveness by fostering educational excellence and ensuring equal access.

Bibliography

Books

Derek Bok — *Higher Education in America.* Princeton, NJ: Princeton University Press, 2013.

Dennis Deslippe — *Protesting Affirmative Action: The Struggle over Equality After the Civil Rights Revolution.* Baltimore, MD: Johns Hopkins University Press, 2012.

Steven Farron — *The Affirmative Action Hoax: Diversity, the Importance of Character, and Other Lies.* Oakton, VA: New Century Foundation, 2010.

Daniel Golden — *The Price of Admissions: How America's Ruling Class Buys Its Way into Elite Colleges—and Who Gets Left Outside the Gates.* New York: Three Rivers Press, 2007.

Christopher Hayes — *Twilight of the Elite: America After Meritocracy.* New York: Crown Publishing, 2012.

Richard D. Kahlenberg, ed. — *Affirmative Action for the Rich: Legacy Preferences in College Admissions.* New York: The Century Foundation Press, 2010.

Bruce P. Lapenson — *Affirmative Action and the Meanings of Merit.* Lanham, MD: University Press of America, 2009.

Patricia Marin and Catherine L. Horn, eds.	*Realizing Bakke's Legacy: Affirmative Action, Equal Opportunity, and Access to Higher Education.* Sterling, VA: Stylus Publishing, 2008.
Jamillah Moore	*Race and College Admissions: A Case for Affirmative Action.* Jefferson, NC: McFarland, 2005.
Julie J. Park	*When Diversity Drops: Race, Religion, and Affirmative Action in Higher Education.* New Brunswick, NJ: Rutgers University Press, 2013.
Barbara A. Perry	*The Michigan Affirmative Action Cases.* Lawrence: University Press of Kansas, 2007.
Peter Sacks	*Tearing Down the Gates: Confronting the Class Divide in American Education.* Berkeley: University of California Press, 2007.
Richard Sander and Stuart Taylor Jr.	*Mismatch: How Affirmative Action Hurts Students It's Intended to Help and Why Universities Won't Admit It.* New York: Basic Books, 2012.
Robert J. Sternberg	*College Admissions for the 21st Century.* Cambridge, MA: Harvard University Press, 2010.
Mitchell L. Stevens	*Creating a Class: College Admissions and the Education of Elites.* Cambridge, MA: Harvard University Press, 2007.

Arvin Vohra

Lies, Damned Lies, and College Admissions: An Inquiry into Education. Irvine, CA: Roland Media Distribution, 2012.

Periodicals and Internet Sources

Michael Barone

"Cheating Is Rife in Colleges—by Admissions Officers," *Washington Examiner*, August 9, 2013.

Kevin Carey

"The Next Affirmative Action: Want to Help Minority College Students? Make the Entire Higher Education System More Accountable," *Washington Monthly*, January–February 2013.

Terry Eastland

"Stop Discriminating," *The Weekly Standard*, July 8, 2013.

Economist

"Unequal Protection: Affirmative Action," April 27, 2013.

Marybeth Gasman and Julie Vultaggio

"A 'Legacy' of Racial Injustice in American Higher Education," *Diverse: Issues in Higher Education*, January 24, 2008.

Michele Hernandez

"Athletes Are the Problem," *New York Times*, November 13, 2011.

William P. Hoar

"'Affirmative' Racism Is Challenged," *The New American*, November 5, 2012. www.thenewamerican.com.

Scott Jaschik — "New Research on 'Mismatch' Released Day After Justice Thomas Cites the Theory to Criticize Affirmative Action," *Inside Higher Ed*, June 26, 2013. www.insidehighered.com.

Richard D. Kahlenberg — "10 Myths About Legacy Preferences in College Admissions," *Chronicle of Higher Education*, September 22, 2010.

Heather Mac Donald — "Affirmative Disaster: A Duke Study Documents the Harm Racial Preferences in College Admissions Can Do to the Intended Beneficiaries," *The Weekly Standard*, February 20, 2012.

Ivan Maisel — "What It Takes," *Stanford Magazine*, November/December 2013. https://alumni.stanford.edu/get/page/magazine/home.

Ashley McDonnell and Alexandra Macfarlane — "Athletes Struggle Against 'Dumb Jock' Stereotype," *Brown Daily Herald*, April 24, 2012. www.browndailyherald.com.

Jonathan Meer and Harvey Rosen — "Family Bonding with Universities," *Research in Higher Education*, November 2010.

Sophie Quinton — "The $6 Envelope That Gets Low-Income Kids into College," *National Journal*, July 16, 2013. www.nationaljournal.com.

Peter Schmidt   "Researchers Accuse Selective
                             Colleges of Giving Admissions Tests
                             Too Much Weight," *Chronicle of
                             Higher Education*, May 9, 2008.

Marjorie Hansen   "Always Have a Backup," *USA Today
Shaevitz   Magazine*, March 2013.

Neal Smatresk   "A Successful Sports Program
                             Benefits Both the University and Our
                             Community," *Las Vegas Sun*,
                             November 11, 2011.

Elizabeth Stoker   "The 1 Percent's Ivy League
and Matthew   Loophole," *Salon*, September 9, 2013.
Bruenig   www.salon.com.

Valerie Strauss   "Reaction to Supreme Court Ruling
                             on Affirmative Action in College
                             Admissions," *Washington Post*, June
                             24, 2013.

Ron Unz   "The Myth of American
                             Meritocracy," *The American
                             Conservative*, November 28, 2012.

Marian Wang   "The Admission Arms Race: Six Ways
                             Colleges Game Their Numbers,"
                             ProPublica, April 23, 2013.
                             www.propublica.org.

Index

A

G

H

I

J